Volatility and Growth

Volatility and Growth

PHILIPPE AGHION
and
ABHIJIT BANERJEE

OXFORD
UNIVERSITY PRESS

OXFORD
UNIVERSITY PRESS

Great Clarendon Street, Oxford OX2 6DP

Oxford University Press is a department of the University of Oxford.
It furthers the University's objective of excellence in research, scholarship,
and education by publishing worldwide in

Oxford New York

Auckland Cape Town Dar es Salaam Hong Kong Karachi
Kuala Lumpur Madrid Melbourne Mexico City Nairobi
New Delhi Shanghai Taipei Toronto

With offices in

Argentina Austria Brazil Chile Czech Republic France Greece
Guatemala Hungary Italy Japan Poland Portugal Singapore
South Korea Switzerland Thailand Turkey Ukraine Vietnam

Oxford is a registered trade mark of Oxford University Press
in the UK and in certain other countries

Published in the United States
by Oxford University Press Inc., New York

British Library Cataloguing in Publication Data
Data available

Library of Congress Cataloging in Publication Data
Data available

Typeset by Newgen Imaging Systems (P) Ltd., Chennai, India
Printed in Great Britain
on acid-free paper by
Biddles Ltd., King's Lynn, Norfolk

ISBN 0-19-924861-3   978-0-19-924861-2

1 3 5 7 9 10 8 6 4 2

To our parents,
Gaby and Raymond Aghion,
and
Nirmala and Dipak Banerjee

Preface

This book grew out of the Clarendon lectures given in Oxford in February 1999. That it took such a long time to turn the lectures into a book, is partly because in 1999 we were still far from any serious analysis of the effects of things that cause volatility on growth (the subject of chapters 1 and 2). Moreover, the material on endogenous volatility in open economies and our third generation model of currency crises, took a while to mature and meet the publication test.

In any case, finishing a book is always hard and this one might indeed be further from the ideal than most. Yet, we now feel that our six chapters convey a consistent message: namely, that in order to understand macroeconomic volatility and growth and the interplays between the two, one needs to start with a vision of an economy where there are "Schumpeterian" entrepreneurs who invest, innovate, and finance their investments through borrowing from a financial sector which is often underdeveloped, and which, as a result, limits them in how much financing they are able to get. It is the interplay of innovative entrepreneurs' needs for financing and the financial sector's willingness to finance them that generates the forces that we study in this book.

The book grew of the confluence of our intellectual histories: One of us had been working on Schumpeterian entrepreneurs for a long time, while the other was interested in imperfections in the credit market. About ten years ago we decided to join forces in order to combine the two, so as to understand better the issues that had to with volatility and growth. The first step in this project, was the material in Chapter 3, which we developed with Thomas Piketty. The material in Chapters 4 and 5 was subsequently developed with Philippe Bacchetta. Finally, the material in Chapters 1 and 2 came out of our collaboration with Marios Angeletos and Kalina Manova. We learned so much from working with Thomas, Philippe, Marios, and Kalina on all these projects, and our debt towards them is enormous.

We also greatly benefited from the views and ideas of Bill East-
erly, Robert King, Larry Jones, Patrick Francois, Huw Llyod-Ellis,
Sergio Rebelo, and Klaus Walde on the effects of volatility on
growth, from our previous collaboration with Gilles Saint-Paul on
the opportunity cost effect of recessions, from the pioneering work
of Ben Bernanke and Mark Gertler on the financial accelerator and
that of Nobu Kyiotaki and John Moore on credit cycles, and from
the work of Olivier Jeanne and Jean Tirole, and the seminal contri-
butions of Paul Krugman, Maurice Obstfeld, and Kenneth Rogoff
on financial crises and open macroeconomics.

This book would not have been if Jim Malcomson and Andrew
Schuller had not initiated it by inviting us to give Clarendon
lectures on volatility and growth, if Andrew Schuller had not followed up and monitored the project through all these years, and
if Jennifer Wilkinson had not been so effective at supervising the
editing, production, and publication process. They all deserve our
deepest thanks.

Miriam Bruhn has performed a fantastic job at turning our messy
notes into polished chapters and at editing and proof-reading the
document at various stages up to completion.

Finally, we are grateful to our spouses, Tuli and Beatriz, for
their unconditional support and immense patience through those
ten years.

Contents

Introduction

ECONOMISTS, going back to Karl Marx, have been interested in the connection between the dynamism of capitalist economies and their apparent instability, marked by the recurrence of the business cycle. For Marx, it all comes out of the mad orgy of accumulation that results from unregulated greed: The economy is driven higher and higher, till it, as it were, topples over.

The economists of the real business cycle school (see Kydland and Prescott 1982; Long and Plosser 1987, for the classic formulations of this view), very far from Marx in almost every other way, share with him a belief that these fluctuations are an integral part of the growth process. In their world, markets always do the best that is possible, given the resource constraints that the economy faces, and therefore fluctuations happen because they have to. The reason why they do, in this view, is that productivity grows in fits and starts, mostly because big new ideas drive productivity and big new ideas are rare. Periods of rapid growth are often followed by a lull, and occasionally, a negative productivity shock (such as an oil shock), so that the entire process looks like a series of fluctuations around an upward trend. Trying to get rid of these fluctuations may come at the cost of killing growth.

Traditional Keynesians hold that there is nothing necessary about many of the ups and downs that we observe: Appropriately chosen policies would get rid of most of them. In their world, however, it is assumed that these fluctuations have nothing to do with growth, which has its own autonomous dynamic.

This monograph grew out of our dissatisfaction with all of these positions. With the Keynesians, for not taking the question seriously: After all, the key insight of modern growth theory is that growth happens through the decisions of individuals and it is hard to imagine that these decisions are entirely insulated from forces that cause the business cycle.[1] With the real business cycle school, in part because our reading of the micro evidence radically undermines their presumption that markets always work, and partly because the data suggests that there are not enough identifiable productivity shocks of the right magnitude to explain by themselves the many ups and downs of capitalist economies. And with the Marxists, because they posit that capitalists would necessarily be driven toward over-accumulation, without identifying the market failure that drives them to do so.

We set out to build a model of the aggregate economy that takes the interactions between volatility and growth seriously, while being open to the possibility of market failures. Specifically, we begin by building a model of macro fluctuations and growth along conventional lines, where growth is driven by R&D and productivity is subject to shocks. What we add is the possibility of imperfections in the credit markets. There is mounting evidence that credit markets, especially in developing countries, but even in the developed world, do not come anywhere close to the neoclassical ideal of a single market rate at which anyone can borrow or lend as much as they want.

We introduce credit market imperfections into the model very simply: We assume that there is a limit to how much credit anyone can get, which is a multiple of their wealth. We allow this multiple to vary across economies, and use it as a natural measure of financial development. A justification for assuming that individuals face a constraint of this kind, including a simple model that generates exactly this kind of credit supply function, is given in Chapter 0.

Chapter 1 starts the main body of the monograph. We investigate what happens when we introduce productivity shocks respectively into the AK model and the Schumpeterian model of endogenous growth. We argue that the main message from both of them is that if volatility has an effect on growth, it is probably positive: it encourages precautionary savings in the AK model, and slumps reduce the opportunity cost of long-term R&D investments in the

---

[1] As Nicholas Kaldor, a Keynesian and a critic, would already comment in the mid-1950s: "As a pure cyclical model, the oscillator model had little resemblance to the cyclical fluctuations in the real world, where successive booms carry production to successively higher levels."

Schumpterian model. Moreover, when volatility hurts growth in the AK model, it is because it leads to lower total investment.

The problem is that in the cross-country data the correlation between volatility and growth is clearly negative (Ramey and Ramey 1995). Moreover, volatility hurts growth even if we control for the investment rate—in other words, it is not simply that volatility hurts total investment.

Chapter 2 introduces credit constraints into the Schumpeterian model developed in Chapter 1. Firms that face credit constraints run the risk that they may not necessarily be able to raise money for profitable investments. In an environment where productivity shocks create uncertainty in a firm's liquidity position, this can discourage firms from undertaking long-term investments that might generate a call on the firm's liquidity. If long-term investment (like R&D) are the investments that generate productivity growth, a combination of shocks and credit constraints can undermine growth.

The theoretical part of Chapter 2 demonstrates this formally, and argues that these effects are large enough to explain a substantial reduction in the growth rate in the most financially underdeveloped countries. The empirical part shows that the correlation between growth and volatility is indeed more negative in the less financially developed countries. Moreover, productivity shocks have a bigger impact on growth in these countries.

So far the presumption has been that the sources of volatility are given from outside, though their effect may be accentuated by credit constraints. The next two chapters set out to investigate whether there can be volatility in this world without any shocks. Chapter 3 shows that this kind of intrinsic volatility can arise in a closed economy if credit constraints are tight but not too tight: The economy does not settle down to a steady state, but fluctuates forever around a trend growth rate, even when there are no shocks. Periods of fast growth tend to push up interest rates, which squeezes profits. As profits shrink, investment falls, because firms are credit constrained and their investment is constrained by how much money they have at hand. This slows growth, which allows profits to be reconstituted, and so on.

This can only happen at certain levels of financial development. In the most developed economies, credit constraints are too slack to matter. These economies grow the fastest and do not fluctuate.

In the least developed ones, they are so tight that growth is always slow and the cycle never starts. These economies do not fluctuate either, but grow slower than the economies at an intermediate level of financial development, which do fluctuate. The idea that it is the economies at an intermediate level of financial development that are most likely to be endogenously volatile carries over to open economies as well. This is the subject of Chapter 4, which should be read as an application of the ideas in Chapter 3 to a specific context where it is easy to match up the theory with the data: The empirical discussion in Chapter 4, largely based on Gourinchas-Valdes-Landeretche (2001), referred to as GVL in the Chapter, suggests that the mechanism underlying our model of endogenous fluctuations matches up well with GVL empirical findings concerning lending booms.

At the heart of these endogenous fluctuations is the idea that shocks, positive or negative, to the borrowing capacity of firms have spillovers on the rest of the economy. An extreme version of what such spillovers can do is a self-fulfilling currency crisis. These happen when people expect a currency crisis and therefore expect the interest cost of foreign currency loans to go up. This leads them to cut back on production, precipitating the crisis. This possibility is the subject of Chapter 5, which also looks at the role of monetary policy in dealing with financial crises in open economies.

0

Modeling Credit Markets

ONE of the core assumptions of the neoclassical model is that there is a single market interest rate and every firm invests to the point where their marginal product is equal to this rate. There is now a large body of research showing, from many different directions, that this neoclassical postulate often does a very poor job of describing reality.

Perhaps the most direct evidence comes from attempts to estimate the marginal product of capital. McKenzie and Woodruff (2003) estimate parametric and nonparametric relationships between firm earnings and firm capital in Mexico. Their estimates suggest that the return on capital for firms with less than US $200 invested is of the order of 15% per month. For firms with investment between US $200 and US $500 the return is between 7% and 10% per month, and it goes down to 5% for firms with investment between US $500 and US $1,000. All of these are well above the informal interest rates available in this area in pawn shops or through micro-credit programs (on the order of 3% per month). In other words, none of the estimated marginal products are equal to each other or to the rate that best approximates the market interest rate.

There are however obvious methodological issues with studies of this kind. First, the investment levels are likely to be correlated with omitted variables. For example, in a world where people can borrow as much as they want, investment will be positively correlated with the expected returns to investment, generating a positive "ability bias" (Olley and Pakes 1996). McKenzie and Woodruff attempt to control for managerial ability by including the firm owner's wage in previous employment, but this may only go a part of the way if individuals choose to enter self-employment precisely because their expected productivity in self-employment is much larger than their productivity in an employed job.[1]

---

[1] There is also direct evidence of very high rates of returns on productive investment in agriculture. Goldstein and Udry (1999) estimate the rates of returns to the production of pineapple in Ghana. The rate of returns associated with switching

Others take a more indirect approach to this problem. An implication of a firm equating its marginal product to the market interest rate is that the firm's investment will be independent of how much money the firm has at hand. In a series of papers, Fazzari *et al.* (1988) test these implications by looking at the impact of shocks to a firm's cash flow on its investment (see Fazzari *et al.* 1988, for example). They find that shocks to cash flow have a consistently positive effect on the firm's investment.

However, this approach has its own problems. The main issue is whether shocks to cash flow are proxying for shocks to the firm's productivity. Fazzari *et al.* (1988) show that their results do not change when they include controls for the firm's market value, which ought to pick up any changes in the firm's productivity. A concern remains however that the market may not know everything that one needs to know about the firm's productivity.

Lamont (1997) addresses this issue by using cash flow shocks that come from an identifiable source, namely shocks to the price of crude oil. He then looks at what happens to the non-oil investments of companies that own an oil company and finds a strong cash flow effect. However, given how big the oil companies are, it is possible that this response has nothing to do with credit constraints, but rather reflects managerial behavior in the presence of "free cash flow."

Banerjee and Duflo (2004) take a yet different approach. They observe that an implication of being unconstrained in the credit market in the sense of being able to borrow as much as you want at the market rate, is that the inflow of subsidized credit into a firm should cause the firm to pay down its nonsubsidized debt, before undertaking additional investment. A constrained firm, by contrast, will want to put what it gets into fresh investments, because its marginal product of capital is higher than the market rate.

To operationalize this strategy they take advantage of a change in the definition of the so-called "priority sector" in India to generate a "natural experiment." All banks in India are required to lend at least 40% of their net credit to the "priority sector," which

---

from the traditional maize and cassava intercrops to pineapple is estimated to be in excess of 1,200%! Few people grow pineapple, however, and this figure may hide some heterogeneity between those who have switched to pineapple and those who have not.

includes small-scale industry, at an interest rate that is required to be no more than 4% above their prime lending rate. In January 1998, the limit on total investment in plants and machinery for a firm to be eligible for inclusion in the small-scale industry category was raised from Rs 6.5 million to Rs 30 million. Banerjee and Duflo first show that, after the reforms, newly eligible firms (those with investment between Rs 6.5 million and 30 million) received on average larger increments in their working capital limit than smaller firms, both in absolute terms and relative to preexisting trends. They then show that the sales and profits increased faster for these firms during the same period. In particular, sales increased almost as fast as credit, suggesting that almost no one is using the extra money to pay down their debt. Most firms appear to be credit constrained.

Banerjee and Duflo then use the variation in the eligibility rule over time to construct instrumental variable estimates of the impact of working capital on sales and profits. The elasticity of profit with respect to working capital is almost 2. Using this and making allowances for the subsidy element in the cost of capital, they estimate that the returns to capital in these firms must be at least 90%. The market interest faced by these firms is certainly no more than 3% per month (43% per year), which is consistent with the rest of the evidence on the firm's being credit constrained.

There seems to be clear evidence that the typical firm, at least in the developing world, has a marginal product which is substantially above the market interest rate. This suggests that the firm cannot borrow as much as it wants at the going market rate. In other words, the supply curve of capital to the firm must be upward sloping, or even vertical (a hard limit on how much the firm can borrow).

To end this section we sketch a simple model taken from Aghion *et al.* (1999a) that explains why lenders impose limits on how much firms can borrow.

Consider a borrower who needs to invest $W + L = I$ in a high-yield technology, where W denotes his or her initial wealth and L is his or her requested loan. The interest rate is r. Both the borrower and the lender are risk neutral. The source of capital market imperfection is the possibility that the borrower may choose not to repay. Namely, once the return $F(W + L)$ is realized, the borrower can either repay immediately and get a net income equal to

$F(W + L) - rL$, or he or she can stall. Stalling revenues away from the lender has a cost to the borrower (who has to keep ahead of the lender); let this cost be a fixed proportion τ of the total investment. Finally, whenever the borrower defaults on his or her repayment obligation, the lender may still invest effort into debt collection. Specifically, assume that a lender has a probability p of collecting his or her due repayment rL. Assume $F(W+L) - \tau(W+L) > rL$ (so that if the borrower stalls but is caught, he or she still has enough resources to repay the lender). Also, take r as exogenously given.

For any given p, the borrower faces a choice between honoring the debt contract and getting $F(W+L) - rL$, and stalling and getting an expected income of $F(W + L) - \tau(W + L) - prL$ (because he still gets caught with probablity p). He will choose the more honorable option if and only if

$$F(W + L) - rL \geq F(W + L) - \tau(W + L) - prL,$$

which implies that

$$\tau(W + L) \geq (1 - p)rL.$$

From this it follows that the amount the lender will be prepared to lend (assuming that he wants the borrower to repay) is capped above by

$$L^* = \frac{\tau W}{(1 - p)r - \tau}.$$

The amount lent is proportional to the borrower's wealth, increasing in the cost of stalling, decreasing in the interest rate, and increasing in the probability of making the borrower repay.

However, it is not clear whether it is reasonable to assume that p is exogenously given: Those lenders who have a greater stake in getting the borrower to repay, will presumably try harder, and therefore p will depend on the amount the lender hopes to get back. To capture this idea, assume that once the borrower starts stalling the lender faces a choice: He can guarantee himself a probability p of collecting his or her due payment rL incurring a nonmonetary effort cost $L \cdot C(p)$, where $C(p) = -c \cdot \ln(1 - p)$.

Faced by a borrower who is stalling, the lender will choose p to maximize:

$$rLp + L \cdot c \cdot \ln(1 - p).$$

The optimal choice of p is the one for which

$$r = \frac{c}{1-p},$$

or $r(1-p) = c$. It follows that the credit limit, L^*, will be given by

$$L^* = \frac{\tau W}{c - \tau}.$$

Note that this is proportional to the borrower's wealth, and increasing in τ, the cost of cheating the lender, and decreasing in c, which determines the lender's cost of collection. This model suggests that the ratio of τ to c, representing the ratio of the cost of cheating to the cost of apprehending cheaters, is a natural measure of the level of financial development. Lending, not surprisingly, is increasing in τ/c.

In the rest of the book, when we simply assume that firms are credit constrained, and the constraint takes the form $L \leq \mu W$, where μ is a positive constant that is increasing in the level of financial development, we will have in mind the model in this section.

1

Volatility and Growth: AK versus Schumpeterian Approach

THE modern approach to growth, often called "new growth theory," really consists of two quite distinct theories. One is the so-called AK approach, which emphasizes the role of capital accumulation. It has been known since the work of Solow (1956) that long-run growth through continuing accumulation of capital is only possible if the aggregate production function is not too concave in capital. The AK model is named after a production function which is linear in capital—$y = Ak$—where k represents capital and A is a constant.

The alternative to the AK model is the Schumpeterian model, which emphasizes the role of R&D and productivity-enhancing investments, more generally, in the growth process. Growth persists in this model because it is always rewarding to come up with a new way of doing things, which generates productivity growth.

The goal of this chapter is to review what these two canonical views of growth tell us about how volatility affects growth.

1.1 Volatility and growth: the AK approach

In an AK model where long-run growth is entirely driven by capital accumulation, the average growth rate depends positively on the savings rate. The savings rate in turn is affected by the degree of macroeconomic volatility, however in a way which is a priori ambiguous: (i) increased volatility induces individuals to save more for precautionary reasons, which in turn leads to a higher equilibrium savings rate and therefore a higher average growth rate in this AK model; (ii) higher macroeconomic volatility tends to reduce the risk-adjusted returns on capital accumulation, and therefore individuals' incentives to sacrifice short-run consumption at the expense of investment; this latter effect tends to discourage savings and thus reduce the average growth rate. Which of these two opposing effects dominates, turns out to depend primarily upon the intertemporal elasticity of substitution in individual consumption over time. All we do in the remaining part of this section, is to formalize this argument; our exposition follows Jones *et al.* (2000).

Consider an economy populated by a continuum of individuals who live for an infinite number of periods, and share the same intertemporal utility function:

$$U(c) = \sum_{t \geq 0} \beta^t \frac{c_t^{1-\sigma}}{1-\sigma},$$

where β is the discount factor and

$$e = 1/\sigma$$

is the intertemporal elasticity of substitution of a representative individual (equivalently, σ is her coefficient of relative risk-aversion). There is only one good in the economy, which serves both as capital and for consumption purposes.

In each period t, the representative individual produces final output using capital, according to the stochastic AK technology

$$y_t = Au_t k_t, \tag{1.1}$$

where A is a productivity parameter which is invariant over time, u_t is an aggregate multiplicative productivity shock with mean equal to 1, and k_t is the capital input used to produce final output at date t. Capital fully depreciates after one period, and the capital invested at any date t is equal to the amount of output saved in period $t-1$. Finally, the shocks u_t are independently and identically distributed over time.

In the initial period 0, the representative individual will choose how to divide final output between consumption and investment, by solving the intertemporal maximization program:

$$\max_{\{c_t, k_t\}} E_0 \left[\sum_{t \geq 0} \beta^t \frac{c_t^{1-\sigma}}{1-\sigma} \right]$$

$$s.t.: \ c_t + k_{t+1} \leq y_t = Au_t k_t,$$

where E_0 denotes the expectation, as of date 0, over all subsequent realizations of the aggregate productivity shock.

The first-order conditions for this maximization, can be expressed by the set of Euler equations:

$$c_t^{-\sigma} = \beta E_t\{c_{t+1}^{-\sigma} A u_{t+1}\},$$

where E_t denotes the expectation over the realization of the productivity shock u_t at date t. We are supposed to solve this equation jointly with the budget constraint, $c_t + k_{t+1} \leq A u_t k_t$, to get to the optimal consumption rule.

To get to this solution, let us start with the guess that consumption is a fixed fraction of output:

$$c_t = \varphi A u_t k_t.$$

Substituting this in the Euler equation above, we get

$$(\varphi A u_t k_t)^{-\sigma} = \beta E_t\{(\varphi A u_{t+1} k_{t+1})^{-\sigma} A u_{t+1}\}$$
$$= \beta E_t\{(\varphi A u_{t+1} A u_t k_t (1 - \varphi))^{-\sigma} A u_{t+1}\},$$

which simplifies to

$$\varphi = 1 - \left\{ A^{1-\sigma} \beta E_t \left[u_{t+1}^{1-\sigma} \right] \right\}^{1/\sigma}.$$

Since this is evidently a constant, we see that the linear consumption rule, $c_t = \varphi A u_t k_t$, satisfies the first-order conditions for a maximum.[1]

Given this consumption rule it is easily checked that the expected growth rate of output from one period to the next will be given by

$$g = E\left(\frac{A u_{t+1} k_{t+1}}{A u_t k_t}; u_t\right) = 1 - \varphi = \left\{A\beta E_t \left[u_{t+1}^{1-\sigma}\right]\right\}^{1/\sigma}.$$

We are now able to address the question that this exercise poses: How does the average growth rate g, vary with macroeconomic volatility?

It is easy to see that a mean-preserving spread in the distribution of aggregate productivity shocks $\{u_t\}$, will increase growth if $u_{t+1}^{1-\sigma}$ is convex in u and reduce it otherwise. This in turn hinges on

---

[1] It can be checked that this actually represents a global maximum.

whether the coefficient σ is greater or smaller than 1. Specifically if the intertemporal elasticity of substitution $e = 1/\sigma$ is greater than 1, then $u^{1-\sigma}$ is concave and therefore an increase in volatility reduces expected growth. In this case, the dominant effect of volatility is to reduce the risk-adjusted return on investment and thereby discourage savings. If instead, as appears to be the case from the available data,[2] the intertemporal elasticity of substitution is less than 1, then $u^{1-\sigma}$ is convex and therefore volatility increases expected growth. In this case, the dominant effect of volatility is to increase precautionary savings and growth.

Thus, according to this AK approach, growth should *increase* with volatility for observed values of the intertemporal elasticity of substitution e.

1.2 The Schumpeterian approach

A second approach to volatility and growth emphasizes the distinction between short-run capital investments and long-term productivity-enhancing investments. Examples of such long-term investments include R&D, IT equipment, and organizational capital. A reason why recessions may have a positive effect on the more long-run investments was suggested by Schumpeter himself: "[Recessions] are but temporary. They are the means to reconstruct each time the economic system on a more efficient plan." Put in more contemporary language, (long-run) productivity-enhancing investments often take place at the expense of directly productive activities. Because the return to the latter is lower in recessions due to lower demand, the opportunity cost of long-run productivity-enhancing investments is lower. Hence the possibility of a growth-enhancing effect of recessions.

This "opportunity cost" argument was first spelled out by Hall (1991), who constructed a model where a constant labor force is allocated between production and the creation of organizational capital (in contrast to real business cycle models where the

---

[2] Hall (1988) finds that the intertemporal elasticity of substitution is smaller than 0.1 and may be 0. Beaudry (1996) uses US state panel data to show that it is not 0, but close to 1.

choice of activities is between production and leisure). Hall writes, "Measured output may be low during [recession] periods, but the time spent reorganizing pays off in its contribution to future productivity." Subsequent work by Bean (1990), Gali and Hammour (1991), and Saint-Paul (1993) looked for empirical evidence supporting the existence of the opportunity cost effect.[3]

1.2.1 Basic framework

The following model is directly drawn from Aghion–Angeletos–Banerjee–Manova (AABM) (2004). Time is discrete and indexed by t. Suppose that at each date t, aggregate productivity A_t fluctuates around a benchmark level T_t which we refer to as the stock of knowledge at date t. We denote by a_t the ratio A_t/T_t: A low value of a_t corresponds to a bad productivity shock. In the absence of aggregate volatility, productivity would coincide with the level of knowledge, namely: $A_t = T_t$. We introduce aggregate volatility in the model by letting

$$\ln A_t = \ln T_t + \ln a_t, \tag{1.2}$$

where a_t represents an exogenous productivity (or demand) shock in period t.[4]

There is a continuum of two-period lived entrepreneurs, which are all *ex ante* identical. Entrepreneurs are risk neutral and consume only in the last period of their lives. Each entrepreneur born in each period t has initial wealth (or human capital endowment equivalent to the amount of wealth) and this wealth is proportional

---

[3] Using a VAR estimation method on a cross-OECD panel data set, Saint-Paul (1993) showed that the effect of demand fluctuations on productivity growth is stronger when demand fluctuations are more transitory.

[4] As in RBC (Real Business Cycle) models, the shock is assumed to follow a random process of the form

$$\ln a_t = \rho \ln a_{t-1} + \varepsilon_t, \tag{1.3}$$

where ε_t is normally distributed with mean equal to $(-\sigma^2/2)$ and variance equal to σ^2 (so that the expectation of the productivity level A_t is equal to the level of knowledge T_t). The parameters $\rho \in [0, 1)$ and $\sigma > 0$ measure respectively the persistence and volatility of the exogenous aggregate shock. Note that T_t can be interpreted as the "trend" in productivity.

to the aggregate level of knowledge, T_t. Let $w = W_t/T_t$ denote the (constant) knowledge-adjusted wealth of an individual at birth.

In the first period of his or her life, the entrepreneur must decide on how to allocate his or her initial wealth endowment between short-run capital investments, K_t, and long-term investments, Z_t. To ensure a balanced-growth path, we assume that, like for initial wealth, the costs of the two types of investments are also proportional to current knowledge T_t, and therefore the relevant variables in our model will be $k_t = K_t/T_t$, and $z_t = Z_t/T_t$, the knowledge-adjusted holdings of capital and R&D investments respectively. The entrepreneur therefore faces a budget constraint (we eliminate i subscripts since all entrepreneurs are *ex ante* identical):

$$k_t + z_t \leq w.$$

Short-run capital investment at date t generates income

$$\Pi_t = A_t(k_t)^\alpha; \quad 0 < \alpha < 1,$$

at the end of the same period. Thus, in the short run, the entrepreneur produces according to a completely standard Cobb–Douglas production technology with productivity parameter A_t.

The interesting part of the model comes from long-term investments: Long-term investment at date t generates income at date $t + 1$ only if the firm can meet some additional liquidity needs that arise at the end of period t. These costs arise either because the project itself needs some additional investments or because the owner of the firm needs to deal with some other problems before he is ready to realize the returns from his long-term investments. Thus, there may be a health crisis that needs to be dealt with before he can focus on the new project. Or there may be a problem in his established busines, which needs to be fixed before he can expect to do anything new. In all of these cases, he needs to spend additional money, the magnitude of which remains unknown until the end of period t. Like all other variables, this cost, $C_t = c_t T_t$, is assumed to be proportional to the current knowledge level T_t, and we denote by c_t the knowledge-adjusted liquidity needs of long-term investment. The realization of this cost is uncertain at the point when the entrepreneur decides on how to allocate her wealth between short- and long-term investment.

The initial long-term investment pays off in period $t + 1$, but only if liquidity needs have been met. In this case the entrepreneur recoups her liquidity needs and, in addition, realizes the long-term profit in period $t + 1$:

$$\Pi_{t+1} = V_{t+1}(z_t)^{\alpha},$$

where $q(z_t) = (z_t)^{\alpha}$ is the probability that the long-term investment is successful and V_{t+1} is the value of a new innovation (which we spell out below). If the entrepreneur can cover the liquidity needs of long-term investment, he or she innovates and recoups the cost, or he or she cannot meet that cost, in which case the productivity remains unchanged in period $t + 1$.

Now, we turn our attention to growth and the dynamics of knowledge over time. As in other models of endogenous technical progress,[5] only the long-term investments, z_t, contribute to long-run growth, with knowledge accumulating over time at a rate proportional to the aggregate rate of innovation in the economy. Namely:

$$g_t \equiv \ln T_{t+1} - \ln T_t = \gamma (z_t)^{\alpha} f_t, \qquad (1.4)$$

where f_t denotes the fraction of entrepreneurs who manage to meet their liquidity needs. In this chapter, we assume perfect capital markets: It will turn out that therefore $f_t = 1$, since once you choose to invest in the long-term project, it always pays to meet the liquidity need. Note that the growth rate of knowledge as defined by (1.4), will certainly vary over time since, z_t, the amount of long-term investment itself fluctuates with the current realization of the productivity shock a_t (we shall see how in a moment).

This long-term investment may be thought of as R&D. However, it is probably more natural to think of it as the starting of a new line of business, or the introduction of a new technology, or the development of a new market.

1.2.2 The opportunity cost effect

Let $v_{t+1} = V_{t+1}/T_t$ denote the knowledge-adjusted final wealth and the knowledge-adjusted value of a new innovation in period $t + 1$. Our main assumption here will be that the returns to long-term investment are less procyclical than the return to capital investments. This amounts to assuming that the correlation

[5] For example, see Romer (1990) or Aghion and Howitt (1992, 1998).

between $v_{t+1} = V_{t+1}/T_t$ and $a_t = A_t/T_t$ over the business cycle is less than one, which, in turn is necessarily the case as long as the productivity shock is less than fully persistent and the value of innovation represents a present value of returns over a horizon extending beyond period t. For simplicity, we shall focus on the special case where the value of innovation only depends upon next period's productivity:

$$V_{t+1} = A_{t+1},$$

which in turn implies that the expected knowledge-adjusted value of an innovation at date $t + 1$, is simply expressed as[6]:

$$\mathbb{E}_t v_{t+1} = (a_t)^\rho. \tag{1.5}$$

In the absence of credit market imperfections, an entrepreneur will always be able to borrow what is necessary in order to cover his or her liquidity needs. This implies that the long-term investment of an entrepreneur in his or her first period of life will always pay out next period in the form of future revenues v_{t+1} from innovating. More formally, consider an entrepreneur born at date t. Her final expected wealth at the end of period $t + 1$ is equal to

$$a_t(k_t)^\alpha + \mathbb{E}_t v_{t+1}(z_t)^\alpha,$$

which the entrepreneur maximizes subject to her budget constraint

$$k_t + z_t \le w.$$

Now, if we concentrate on interior solutions, we obtain the first-order conditions:

$$\alpha a_t(k_t)^{\alpha-1} = \lambda,$$
$$\alpha(z_t)^{\alpha-1}\mathbb{E}_t v_{t+1} = \lambda, \tag{1.6}$$

where λ is the Lagrange multiplier on the budget constraint.

---

[6] $V_{t+1} = A_{t+1}$ implies $v_{t+1} = a_{t+1}$. Now using the AR(1.1) process for a_{t+1} specified in (1.3) we have that $a_{t+1} = a_t^\rho e^{\varepsilon_{t+1}}$. Thus, $\mathbb{E}_t v_{t+1} = a_t^\rho \mathbb{E} e^{\varepsilon_{t+1}} = a_t^\rho e^{-(\sigma^2/2)+(\sigma^2/2)} = a_t^\rho$.

These conditions immediately imply that z_t is countercyclical whereas k_t is procyclical, with:

$$k_t(a_t) = \frac{a_t^\eta}{1 + a_t^\eta}w \quad \text{and} \quad z_t(a_t) = \frac{1}{1 + a_t^\eta}w, \qquad (1.7)$$

where $\eta = (1 - \rho)/(1 - \alpha) > 0$. The intuition is straightforward: Suppose there is a good productivity shock, that is, a high realization of a_t at date t. With such a high productivity level, it is more profitable to invest in short-run production than in long-term investment, which will improve productivity in some future period that will probably be less productive. As a result, long-term investment at date t will be relatively low. Conversely, suppose there is bad productivity shock at date t. Then it becomes more profitable for the entrepreneur to invest in long-term investment. Hence, the countercyclicality of long-term investment: low long-term investment in a boom, high long-term investment in a slump.

This countercyclicality, in turn, has important implications when analyzing the effect of volatility on growth. From the growth equation (1.4), the average growth rate of technology in the long run is equal to:

$$g \equiv E(g_t) = \gamma E_{a_t}((z(a_t))^\alpha).$$

Now, using the fact that $(z_t(a_t))^\alpha = (1/(1 + a_t^\eta)w)^\alpha$, is convex in a_t,[7] we obtain that higher volatility, measured by a mean preserving spread in a_t should translate into a higher expected growth rate g_t. The intuition for the result is shown in Figure 1.1, which pictures the equilibrium innovation probability $(z_t(a_t))^\alpha$ as a function of a_t.

We clearly see that the convexity of this function implies that a mean-preserving spread from perfect certainty over the realization of a_t, increases the average rate of growth-enhancing

---

[7] To see this, note first that $(z(a_t))^\alpha$ is proportional to

$$f(a_t) = (1 + a_t^\eta)^{-\alpha}.$$

Next, we have:

$$f'(a_t) = -\frac{\alpha\eta}{(1 + a_t^\eta)^{\alpha+1}a_t^{1-\eta}},$$

which is obviously increasing in a_t since

$$\eta = (1 - \rho)(1 - \alpha) < 1.$$

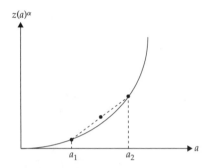

Fɪɢ. 1.1 Equilibrium innovation probability.

Note: If we randomize between a_1 and a_2, the average innovation probability lies strictly above the curve.

investments. Thus, without credit constraints, this opportunity cost model of volatility and growth delivers again the prediction that higher volatility should translate in higher growth. As we shall see in the next section, in spite of the potential suggested above, which points to a potential positive effect of recessions on "organizational capital," the overall cross-country evidence on volatility and growth goes pretty much the other way.

1.3 The existing evidence on volatility and growth

The work of Bruno (1993) on inflation and growth, and later Gavin and Hausmann (1996), and the Inter-American Development Bank report on Volatility in Latin America in the mid-1990s, provides strong cross-country evidence of the detrimental effects of volatility on long-run growth, particularly in countries or the subset of countries with low levels of financial development as measured by the ratio of bank credit to GDP (see Figure 1.2).

The most cited work on the subject is probably the AER paper by Ramey and Ramey (1995), henceforth RR. RR consider cross-sectional data from 92 countries, and regress average growth over aggregate volatility. Annual growth is computed as the log difference of per capita income obtained from the Penn World Tables

Table 1.1 Ramey and Ramey revisited

| | No investment | | | | With investment | | | |
| | Whole sample | | OECD countries | | Whole sample | | OECD countries | |
Independent variable	(1)	(2)	(3)	(4)	(5)	(6)	(7)	(8)
Initial income	-0.0019	-0.0175	-0.0110	-0.0258	-0.0094	-0.0163	-0.0123	-0.0258
	(-0.69)	(-5.66)***	(-3.49)***	(-7.47)***	(-3.89)***	(-5.98)***	(-4.25)***	(-6.99)***
Volatility	-0.2796	-0.2641	0.0370	-0.2939	-0.1829	-0.2208	0.0142	-0.2899
	(-2.63)***	(-2.78)***	(0.22)	(-1.44)	(-2.14)**	(-2.63)**	(0.09)	(-1.33)
Investment/GDP					0.1742	0.0963	0.0662	0.0058
					(6.47)***	(3.96)***	(2.43)**	(0.17)
Pop growth		-0.0085		-0.0011		-0.0075		-0.0008
		(-3.53)***		(-0.39)		(-3.54)***		(-0.25)
Sec school enrollment		0.0116		0.0050		0.0015		0.0047
		(0.89)		(0.90)		(0.13)		(0.77)
Government size		-0.00020		-0.00019		-0.00025		-0.00014
		(-0.58)		(-0.51)		(-0.82)		(-0.29)
Inflation		0.0003		-0.0011		0.0002		-0.0010
		(2.45)**		(-1.83)ʃ		(1.89)*		(-1.07)
Black market premium		-0.0127		-0.0414		-0.0123		-0.0382
		(-1.61)		(-0.44)		(-1.78)*		(-0.37)

Trade openness		0.00012		−0.00008		0.00010		−0.00008
		(2.25)**		(−1.45)		(2.14)**		(−1.30)
Intell property rights		0.0003		−0.0019		0.0004		−0.0018
		(0.14)		(−0.70)		(0.21)		(−0.57)
Property rights		0.0030		0.0004		0.0018		0.0006
		(2.67)***		(0.35)		(1.74)*		(0.37)
R^2	0.0969	0.6018	0.4194	0.9367	0.4472	0.7013	0.5515	0.9370
N	70	59	24	19	70	59	24	19

Note: Dependent variable is average growth over the 1960–95 period. All regressors are averages over the 1960–95 period, except for intellectual and property rights which are for 1970–95 and 1970–90 respectively. Initial income and secondary school enrollment are taken for 1960. Constant term not shown. *T*-statistics in parenthesis. ***, **, *, ^, significant at the 1%, 5%, 10%, and 11% respectively.

Source: AABM (2004), table 1.

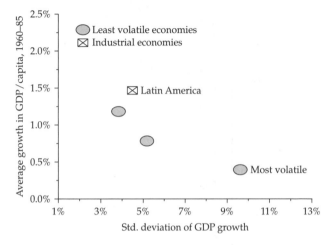

FIG. 1.2 Volatility and growth of real GDP per capita.
Source: Gavin and Hausmann (1996), figure 2.

(PWT) mark 6.1. Aggregate volatility is measured by the country-specific standard deviation of annual growth over the 1960–92 period. In addition RR construct an estimate of the part of the volatility that is due to exogenous shocks, by using a filter to take out the endogenous movements in GDP. Their first finding is that there is a negative correlation between the standard deviation of per capita annual growth rates and the average growth rate. Second, this correlation becomes negligible once the cross-country regression is restricted to OECD countries. Third, they find that the negative correlation between volatility and growth persists when one controls for the ratio of average investment over GDP. These findings, summarized in Table 1.1, are clearly at odds with the theories, based in a world with no credit constraints, that we developed earlier.

In the next chapter we will argue that the RR findings can be easily accounted for by simply introducing credit constraints in the opportunity cost model in the previous section.

2

Financial Development and the Effects of Volatility on Growth

WE argued in Chapter 0 that credit constraints are an important part of life, especially in the developing world. In this chapter we argue, based on Aghion–Angeletos–Banerjee–Manova (AABM), that the presence of credit constraints can help us understand why volatility is so costly for growth.

The basic idea behind our explanation is rather obvious: The long-term productivity-enhancing investment in the model developed in the previous chapter creates a need for liquidity; with perfect credit markets the necessary liquidity is always supplied. Not so with imperfect credit markets: The liquidity shock is only financed when the firm has enough profits, because only profitable firms can borrow a lot. A negative productivity shock, by making firms less profitable, makes it less likely that the liquidity need would not be met. As a result, a fraction of the potentially productivity-enhancing long-term investments will go to waste, with obvious consequences for growth.

An empirical implication of this approach is that countries with better financial markets will deal better with volatility. We test this in a cross-section of 70 countries over the period 1960–95 and find, like RR, a strong direct negative effect of volatility on growth, and that productivity growth is less sensitive to volatility when the degree of financial development is higher. However, it is not clear that this result can be causally interpreted, since volatility is endogenous, and is clearly influenced by the level of financial development. We thus also report panel regressions from AABM of the response of per capita growth to exogenous changes in the terms of trade and an export-weighted measure of price commodity shocks, both annually and at 5-year intervals. Looking at 5-year averages, in a sample of 73 countries between 1960 and 1985 they find that deteriorations in the terms of trade are less harmful to productivity growth in countries with higher financial development. This result is robust to alternative measures of current or lagged credit constraints.

Finally, the model developed in this section predicts that long-term innovative investment should be more cyclical in more credit-constrained economies. Based on an annual panel of 14 OECD countries over the period 1973–97, AABM find that, as predicted by the theory, the ratio of R&D (which is taken as a proxy of long-term investment) over total investment responds more procyclically to lagged commodity–price shocks when the country is at a low level of financial development. On the other hand, total investment as a share of GDP does not respond in any systematic way to commodity–price shocks, suggesting that the effect of shocks on future growth is actually channeled through the reallocations of capital between short-term and long-term investments.

2.1 *Financial development and the effect of volatility on growth*

Let us augment the model of short- versus long-term investment developed in Section 1.3 of the previous chapter by introducing credit market imperfections. Thus, we assume that upon investing in short-run capital and in long-term investments, an entrepreneur born at date t can borrow only up to m times his or her initial wealth, so that he or she faces the investment constraint

$$k_t^i + z_t^i \leq \mu w,$$

where $\mu = 1 + m$.

Similarly, after the realization of the liquidity cost c_t^i on the long-term investment at the end of period t, the entrepreneur can borrow up to μ times his or her end-of-current-period wealth for the purpose of covering these liquidity needs. Thus, his or her initial long-term investment z_t^i at the beginning of period t will pay out in period $t + 1$ if and only if

$$c_t^i \leq x_t^i \equiv \mu a_t \left(k_t^i\right)^\alpha.$$

Thus, the entrepreneur's long-term investment will pay out next period with probability

$$\Pr\left(c_t^i \le x_t^i\right) \equiv F\left(x_t^i\right).$$

Since all entrepreneurs born at date t are *ex ante* identical, for notational simplicity we shall drop the i superscripts. Assuming again for simplicity that the knowledge-adjusted value v_{t+1} of innovating at date $t + 1$, is equal to the knowledge-adjusted productivity a_{t+1} at that date, an entrepreneur born at date t will now choose his or her investment profile (k_t, z_t) so as to:

$$\max_{k,z} \left\{a_t(k_t)^\alpha + \mathbb{E}_t a_{t+1}(z_t)^\alpha F\left(\mu a_t(k_t)^\alpha\right)\right\}$$

$$s.t.: k_t + z_t \le \mu w.$$

Let us concentrate on the special case where

$$\ln F\left(x_t^i\right) \approx \phi \ln x_t^i,$$

where ϕ is the (local) elasticity of F.

Both parameters μ and ϕ reflect the tightness of credit constraints: $\mu = \infty$ corresponds to perfect credit markets, whereas $\mu = 1$ corresponds to the absence of a credit market. More generally, a lower value of μ corresponds to tighter credit constraints or equivalently to a lower degree of financial development. Similarly, $\phi = 0$ means that the probability of surviving the long-term investment liquidity needs is independent of wealth, whereas a large ϕ corresponds to a high wealth sensitivity of this survival probability.

Then, under the above log–linear specification for the distribution function of the liquidity cost c, we obtain the first-order condition[1]:

$$\left(\frac{k_t}{z_t}\right)^{1-\alpha} \approx \frac{a_t^{1-\rho-\phi}}{\left[\mu\,(k_t)^\alpha\right]^\phi} + \phi\left(\frac{z_t}{k_t}\right)^\alpha. \tag{2.1}$$

In particular, we see that z_t/k_t is procyclical if and only if $\phi > 1 - \rho$. Moreover, the procyclicality of z_t increases with a higher ϕ, a lower μ, or a lower ρ. Recall that both μ and ϕ reflect the tightness

---

[1] See AABM for a detailed derivation.

of credit constraints and as we might have expected, z_t falls with
either a reduction in μ or an increase in ϕ.

Using the fact that

$$k_t + z_t = w,$$

in equilibrium (in the absence of foreign lending or government
bonds, and given that all entrepreneurs are *ex ante* identical with
the same initial wealth so that there is no reason why one entrepreneur would end up lending to another entrepreneur in period
t), we thus conclude that *under sufficiently incomplete markets, the
share of R&D z_t becomes procyclical, and the share of capital investment
k_t becomes countercyclical. Long-term investment z_t is less procyclical
the less tight the credit constraints, less persistent the shocks, or longer
the horizon of long-term investment.*

The intuition for why long-term investment becomes more procyclical when credit constraints are tighter, can be explained as
follows: under tight credit constraints, a low realization of current productivity a_t means low level of profits $a_t(k_t)^\alpha$ at the end of
the current period. But, under tight credit constraints, this in turn
implies a low borrowing capacity and therefore a low ability to
respond to the liquidity shock c on the long-term investment, and
therefore it makes it very unlikely that the long-term investment
today at date t will pay out in the future. Anticipating this, an
entrepreneur facing a low productivity shock today will shy away
from long-term investment, hence the procyclicality of long-term
investment under tight credit constraints.

The above reasoning also implies that the tighter the credit constraint, the more risky it is to invest in long-term investments in
general, therefore the lower the mean long-term investment over
time, and consequently the lower the average growth rate.

> EXAMPLE 1: The following two figures show how credit con-
> straints affect the level and procyclicality of long-term invest-
> ment. Here, we assume that the distribution of c is lognormal.
> We also assume that $\alpha = 1/3$, and we let μ vary between 1 (no
> credit) and 5.

Figure 2.1 depicts the equilibrium level of z_t, evaluated at the
mean productivity level ($a_t = 1$). Figure 2.2 depicts the equilibrium

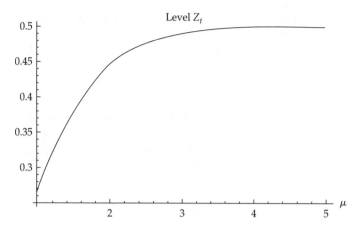

FIG. 2.1 The effect of incomplete markets on the level of long-term investment.

Source: AABM (2004), figure 2.

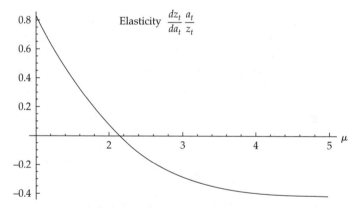

FIG. 2.2 The effect of incomplete markets on the cyclical elasticity of long-term investment.

Source: AABM (2004), figure 3.

cyclical elasticity of z_t (also evaluated at $a_t = 1$). In particular, we see that for μ sufficiently small, z_t is increasing in a_t $((dz_t/da_t) > 0)$: In other words, long-term investment becomes procyclical when μ is small and becomes countercyclical for μ sufficiently large.

We now turn our attention back to the effect of increased volatility on long-run average growth, and how it is affected by credit constraints. In the economy with credit constrained firms, by the law of large number only a fraction,

$$\delta(a_t) \equiv F(\mu a_t(w - z(a_t))^\alpha),$$

of entrepreneurs will successfully meet the liquidity needs of long-term investment.

Now if we assume that knowledge grows at a rate proportional to the number of *implemented* (i.e. *completed*) innovations, then the growth rate of technology is now given by:

$$g_t \equiv \ln T_{t+1} - \ln T_t = \gamma(z(a_t))^\alpha \delta(a_t),$$

where $z(a_t)$ is the (incomplete-markets) equilibrium level of long-term investment. Recall that in the absence of credit constraints (see Chapter 1) we simply had

$$g_t = \gamma(z(a_t))^\alpha,$$

since all innovations were always completed.

In fact, one can show that $(z(a_t))^\alpha \delta(a_t)$ is always concave in a_t under the Cobb–Douglas long-term investment technology considered in this chapter. Thus, the growth rate g_t is a concave function of a_t, and therefore mean growth will now fall in response to an increase in the variance of a_t (see Figure 2.3). Thus, *in an economy with credit-constrained firms, an increase in volatility will result in lower mean growth.*

> EXAMPLE 2: Assume linear production and long-term investment technologies, namely:
>
> $$\pi(k) = ak, \qquad q(z) = \lambda z.$$

Suppose also that the long-term growth-enhancing investment is indivisible, equal to some $z_0 \in (0, w)$, that the distribution for the liquidity shock $\tilde{c}$ is uniform over the interval $[0, 1]$, and that in the absence of volatility, firms could always pay $\tilde{c}$ with their retained earnings from short-run production, more precisely:

$$\bar{a}\pi(k_0) = \bar{a}(w - z_0) \geq 1,$$

where $\bar{a}$ is the average productivity shock.

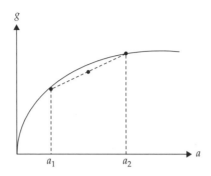

FIG. 2.3 Growth rate under Cobb–Douglas long-term investment technology.

Note: If we randomize between a_1 and a_2, the average growth rate lies strictly below the curve.

We are interested in the effect of increased macroeconomic volatility (i.e. of increased variance of a, denoted by σ) on the expected growth rate

$$g = E_a(\lambda z_0 \delta(a)),$$

where

$$\delta(a) = \Pr(\mu a(w - z_0) \geq \tilde{c}).$$

Since the liquidity shock is uniform, we have:

$$\delta(a) = \delta(a, \mu) = \min(\mu a(w - z_0), 1),$$

which is obviously concave in a. Figure 2.4 shows $\delta(a)$ as a function of a. In particular we see that randomizing between two values of a below and above the kink can only reduce the average δ so that volatility is unambiguously detrimental to average growth.

It then immediately follows that the expected growth rate g must decrease when the variance of a increases, and all the more when μ is lower. This result is quite intuitive: more volatility does not improve firms' ability to overcome the liquidity shock in a boom since firms already do it without volatility. However, it reduces the probability that they will overcome the liquidity shock in a slump, and to a larger extent when the firm faces tighter borrowing

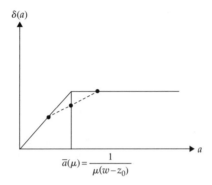

FIG. 2.4 Volatitlity is detrimental to average growth.

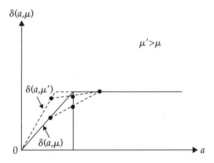

FIG. 2.5 Increased access to credit reduces the sensitivity of growth to productivity shocks.

constraints. We thus have:

$$\frac{\partial g}{\partial \sigma} < 0 \quad \text{and} \quad \frac{\partial^2 g}{\partial \sigma \partial \mu} > 0.$$

Moreover, the *ex post* growth rate,

$$\lambda z_0 \delta(a),$$

is increasing and concave in a, but becomes constant and equal to λz_0 when μ is sufficiently large. Thus growth reacts positively to favorable productivity shocks and at the same time more volatility is detrimental to growth. Now, Figure 2.5 depicts $\delta(a) = \delta(a, \mu)$ for two values of μ, namely μ and $\mu' > \mu$. We see that a negative shock on a has a less detrimental effect for μ' than for μ.

Thus, increased access to credit (a higher μ) reduces the sensitivity of growth to productivity shocks and also the extent to which volatility is detrimental to growth (since growth becomes less concave in a).

2.1.1 Main theoretical predictions

To complete this section we list our main predictions as they emerge from our above discussion:

1. Long-term investment tends to be countercyclical in the absence of credit constraints, but becomes increasingly procyclical as credit constraints tighten.
2. When firms face tighter credit constraints, the effect of volatility on expected average growth tends to become more negative (or less positive).
3. When firms face tighter constraints, growth becomes more sensitive to exogenous shocks.

2.2 Empirical analysis

In the rest of this section we present, based on AABM, some results from trying to test the above predictions.

2.2.1 Data and measurement

Annual growth is computed as the log difference of per capita income obtained from the Penn World Tables (PWT) mark 6.1. As in Ramey and Ramey (1995), aggregate volatility is measured by taking the country-specific standard deviation of annual growth over the 1960–95 period.

Financial development is measured by the ratio of private credit, that is the value of loans by financial intermediaries to the private sector, over GDP. Data for 71 countries on 5-year interval averages between 1960 and 1995 (1960–4, 1965–9, etc.) was first compiled by Levine *et al.* (2000); an annual dataset was more recently prepared and made available by Levine on his webpage. Private credit is the preferred measure of financial development by Levine *et al.* because it excludes credit granted to the public sector and funds coming from central or development banks. AABM also conduct sensitivity analysis with two alternative measures of credit constraints: liquid liabilities and bank assets. The first is defined as currency plus demand and interest-bearing liabilities of banks and nonbank financial intermediaries divided by GDP; the second gives the value of all loans by banks but not other financial intermediaries.

The next step in presenting the evidence is to look at the response of growth to specific shocks. AABM first consider terms of trade shocks, available as 5-year averages between 1960 and 1985 from the Barro-Lee (1996) dataset. Changes in the terms of trade reflect export-weighted changes in export prices net of import-weighted changes in import prices, quoted in the same currency. Arguably, exchange rate fluctuations may be endogenous to the growth process and therefore regressions of growth on terms of trade shocks may be subject to reverse causality and produce biased coefficient estimates. AABM therefore also construct an annual index of export-weighted commodity price shocks using data on the international prices of 42 products between 1960 and 2000 available from the International Financial Statistics (IFS) Database of the IMF.

For the analysis on the transmission channel of credit constraints, one also needs data on long-term versus short-run investments. AABM consider R&D as a share of total investment. Unfortunately, data availability limits the sample to 14 OECD countries between 1973 and 1997 for which the OECD reports spending on R&D in the ANBERD database. Data on investment as a share of GDP is easily obtainable from the PWT.

In the growth regressions AABM follow Ramey and Ramey and Levine *et al.* in controlling for population growth, initial secondary school enrollment, and a set of four policy variables (the share of government in GDP, inflation, the black market exchange rate premium, and openness to trade). We use demographics data from the PWT and the policy conditioning set in Levine *et al.*

2.2.2 *A summary of the AABM results*

While Ramey and Ramey study the response of long-term growth to volatility and Levine *et al.* focus on the direct effects of credit constraints on growth, our model predicts that volatility is more harmful to long-run growth in financially underdeveloped countries. AABM therefore estimate the basic equation:

$$g_i = \alpha_0 + \alpha_1 \cdot y_i + \alpha_2 \cdot \text{vol}_i + \alpha_3 \cdot \text{priv}_i$$
$$+ \alpha_4 \cdot \text{vol}_i * \text{priv}_i + \beta \cdot X_i + \varepsilon_i,$$

where y_i is the initial income in country i, g_i denotes the average rate of productivity growth in country i over the whole period 1960–95, vol_i is the measure of aggregate volatility, priv_i is the average measure of financial development over the period 1960–95, X_i is a vector of country-specific controls, and ε_i is the noise term. We are mostly interested in the interaction term $\alpha_4 \cdot \text{vol}_i * \text{priv}_i$, and our first prediction is that α_4 should be positive and significant. We also believe that α_2 should be negative and significant, so that volatility is negatively correlated with growth in countries with low financial development, but less so when financial development increases.

Table 2.1 presents the results reported in AABM. They find a strong direct negative effect of volatility on long-term growth of -0.41 and a significant positive coefficient on the interaction term of 0.011 (Column (1)). In this sample private credit varies from 4% to 141%, with a mean of 38% and a standard deviation of 29%. A one standard deviation increase in the level of financial development would therefore reduce the impact of a 1% rise in volatility from a 0.41% fall in the growth rate to $-0.41 + 0.011 * 29 = -0.09\%$. This effect is significant in economic terms not only because of the large variation in private credit in the cross-section, but also because of its substantial fluctuations in the time series: For example, in the United States private credit almost tripled between 1960 and 1995, steadily rising from 50% to 140%. For many countries the level of private credit moved up and down significantly during the same period. As Column (2) shows, the AABM result is robust to the inclusion of demographic and human capital controls, as well as measures of property rights protection and the policy variables from Levine *et al.*

For sufficiently high levels of private credit (which we observe for many OECD countries) these results predict that the overall contribution of volatility to economic growth becomes positive. Moreover, for intermediate levels of private credit the gross contribution may be close to zero. Regressing long-run growth on

Table 2.1 Growth, volatility, and credit constraints: basic specification

Independent variable	No investment				With investment			
	Whole sample		OECD countries		Whole sample		OECD countries	
	(1)	(2)	(3)	(4)	(5)	(6)	(7)	(8)
Initial income	−0.0071	−0.0174	−0.0177	−0.0256	−0.0103	−0.0159	−0.0173	−0.0256
	(−2.56)**	(−5.77)***	(−6.69)***	(−6.32)***	(−4.10)***	(−5.70)***	(−6.55)***	(6.01)***
Volatility	−0.4129	−0.5098	−0.5165	−0.5196	−0.3012	−0.4245	−0.5446	−0.5607
	(−3.06)***	(−3.33)***	(−1.73)*	(−1.14)	(−2.52)**	(−2.98)***	(−1.83)*	(−1.16)
Private credit	−0.00005	−0.00016	−0.00019	−0.00006	−0.00008	−0.00020	−0.00021	−0.00008
	(−0.29)	(−0.98)	(−1.26)	(−0.29)	(−0.60)	(−1.34)	(−1.39)	(−0.37)
Volatility*private credit	0.0113	0.0090	0.0080	0.0040	0.0069	0.0069	0.0083	0.0049
	(2.59)**	(2.15)**	(1.67)^	(0.63)	(1.76)*	(1.78)*	(1.73)^	(0.72)
Investment/GDP					0.1420	0.0857	0.0270	0.0218
					(4.68)***	(3.20)***	(1.13)	(0.63)
Pop growth		−0.0081		0.0005		−0.0076		0.0018
		(−3.55)***		(0.17)		(−3.64)***		(0.48)
Sec school enrollment		0.0037		0.0064		−0.0040		0.0056
		(0.28)		(1.15)		(−0.33)		(0.92)

	(1)	(2)	(3)	(4)	(5)	(6)	(7)
Government size		−0.00001		0.00006		−0.00013	0.00027
		(−0.04)		(0.14)		(−0.43)	(0.51)
Inflation		0.0003		−0.0004		0.0002	0.0001
		(2.78)***		(−0.52)		(1.91)*	(0.11)
Black market premium		−0.0072		−0.0380		−0.0082	−0.0218
		(0.91)		(−0.34)		(−1.14)	(−0.18)
Trade openness		0.00011		−0.00004		0.00009	−0.00003
		(2.06)**		(−0.62)		(1.98)*	(−0.36)
Intell property rights		0.0013		−0.0015		0.0018	−0.0007
		(0.50)		(−0.50)		(0.76)	(−0.22)
Property rights		0.0023		0.0003		0.0018	0.0009
		(1.94)*		(0.23)		(0.76)	(0.57)
						(1.64)^	
F-test (volatility terms)	0.0103	0.0051	0.2462	0.4122	0.0489	0.0105	0.4580
F-test (credit terms)	0.0001	0.0310	0.0690	0.3993	0.0814	0.2120	0.3875
R^2	0.3141	0.6576	0.7894	0.9534	0.4889	0.7212	0.9569
N	70	59	22	19	70	59	19

Note: Dependent variable is average growth over the 1960–95 period. All regressors are averages over the 1960–95 period, except for intellectual and property rights which are for 1970–95 and 1970–90 respectively. Initial income and secondary school enrollment are taken for 1960. Constant term not shown. T-statistics in parenthesis. P-values from an F-test of the joint significance of volatility terms (volatility and volatility*credit) and credit terms (credit and volatility*credit) reported. ***, **, *, ^ significant at the 1%, 5%, 10%, and 11% respectively.

Source: AABM (2004), table 2.

volatility alone without accounting for the direct and interacted effects of financial development, could thus produce an insignificant coefficient. This may explain why Ramey and Ramey find a strong negative effect of volatility on growth in the full cross-section but a nonsignificant one in the OECD sample. In Columns (3) and (4) AABM estimate the above equation for the OECD countries only, and find coefficients similar to the ones we find for the entire sample.

Finally, Columns (5) and (6) show that the growth impact of both volatility itself and its interaction with private credit are little affected by the inclusion of investment as a control. Risk arguably affects savings rates and investment, and investments fuel growth. However, controlling for the ratio of investment to GDP reduces the coefficient on volatility by only 20%, suggesting that 80% of the total effect of volatility on growth is via a channel other than the rate of investment.

These results have been shown to be robust to alternative measures of financial development, namely liquid liabilities and bank assets.[2]

Next, to address the potential endogeneity problem raised by the above measure of volatility, AABM analyze the sensitivity of growth to exogenous shocks, exploring both the cross-section and time-series variation in the panel. They consider average data over 5-year period intervals in a cross-section of over 70 countries to estimate the following specification:

$$g_{it} = \alpha_0 + \alpha_1 \cdot y_{it} + \alpha_2 \cdot \text{shock}_{it} + \alpha_3 \cdot \text{priv}_{it}$$
$$+ \alpha_4 \cdot \text{shock}_{it} * \text{priv}_{it} + \beta \cdot X_{it} + \mu_i + \varepsilon_{it},$$

where g_{it} and priv_{it} are the annual growth and private credit averages for country i in the 5-year subperiod t, and y_{it} is the initial per capita income at the beginning of the subperiod. To measure the shock term, shock_{it}, we consider both the average terms-of-trade shock and the average commodity price shock during the subperiod. We expect a positive terms-of-trade shock to stimulate growth, and therefore α_2 to be positive. Similarly, we anticipate a positive direct effect of financial development, thus α_3 should

---

[2] See AABM, table 4.

Independent variable	Terms of trade shocks				Price commodity shocks			
	Private credit$_t$		Initial credit	Lagged credit	Private credit$_t$		Initial credit	Lagged credit
	OLS (1)	FE (2)	FE (3)	FE (4)	OLS (5)	FE (6)	FE (7)	FE (8)
Initial income	−0.0063 (−2.02)**	−0.0757 (−8.06)***	−0.0670 (−7.22)***	−0.0899 (−7.12)***	−0.0076 (−2.68)***	−0.0701 (−8.34)***	−0.0592 (−6.92)***	−0.0751 (−7.00)***
Shock	0.1402 (3.07)***	0.1383 (3.60)***	0.1062 (2.31)**	0.1640 (3.65)***	0.1297 (2.43)**	0.1243 (2.68)***	0.1462 (2.45)**	0.1234 (2.36)**
Private credit	0.0143 (1.71)*	0.0177 (1.09)		0.0145 (0.64)	0.0264 (3.61)***	0.0387 (3.21)***		0.0325 (1.99)**
Private credit*shock	−0.3226 (−1.89)*	−0.3509 (−2.24)**	−0.0539 (−0.23)	−0.3599 (−1.78)*	−0.2263 (−1.22)	−0.2119 (−1.33)	−0.4207 (−1.44)	−0.2065 (−0.99)
Controls								
pop growth, sec enroll	yes	yes	yes	yes	yes	yes	yes	yes
R^2	0.0696				0.0867			
R^2 within		0.3296	0.3418	0.3608		0.2723	0.2650	0.2519
R^2 between		0.0419	0.0287	0.0320		0.0403	0.0322	0.0516
# countries (groups)		73	57	70		72	57	72
N	323	323	277	255	388	388	331	321

Note: Dependent variable is average growth over 5-year intervals in the 1960–85 period. Terms of trade shock is defined as the growth of export prices less the growth of import prices. Commodity price shocks are export-weighted changes in the price of 42 commodities. Both shocks are averaged over the corresponding 5-year interval. Private credit is concurrent 5-year average, initial 1960–64 average or lagged (t-5,t-1) average as indicated in the column heading. Constant term not shown. T-statistics in parenthesis. ***, **, *, ^ significant at the 1%, 5%, 10%, and 11% respectively.

Source: AABM (2004), table 4.

Table 2.3 The response of investment to commodity price shocks: annual panel data, fixed effects

Dependent variable:	Investment/GDP				R&D/investment			
Credit and prop rights:	(t-5,t-1) avg		(t-10,t-6) avg		(t-5,t-1) avg		(t-10,t-6) avg	
Independent variable:	(1)	(2)	(3)	(4)	(5)	(6)	(7)	(8)
$Shock_t$	−2.56	−9.19	−27.60	−9.14	0.2629	0.7217	0.5945	0.2863
	(−0.21)	(−0.20)	(−0.59)	(−0.85)	(0.65)	(0.52)	(0.58)	(0.79)
$Shock_{t-1}$	10.06	22.58	47.85	12.61	0.0547	1.0157	0.4940	0.0642
	(0.82)	(0.47)	(1.00)	(1.16)	(0.14)	(0.70)	(0.48)	(0.18)
$Shock_{t-2}$	−7.56	111.51	148.02	−13.19	0.7429	−1.0500	0.0350	0.8298
	(−0.65)	(3.09)***	(3.89)***	(−1.20)	(1.94)*	(−0.97)	(0.04)	(2.24)**
Priv credit	1.83	−0.17	−1.71	5.93	−0.0583	0.0078	−0.0685	−0.0735
	(1.32)	(−0.11)	(−0.77)	(3.72)***	(−1.29)	(0.17)	(−1.41)	(−1.37)
Priv credit*$shock_t$	11.54	9.81	8.43	23.25	−0.3734	−0.2190	−0.2459	−0.4368
	(0.62)	(0.39)	(0.34)	(1.40)	(−0.61)	(−0.29)	(−0.45)	(−0.78)
Priv credit*$shock_{t-1}$	−2.23	0.14	−16.62	−3.42	−0.0871	−0.0220	0.0518	−0.1722
	(−0.12)	(0.01)	(−0.69)	(−0.20)	(−0.14)	(−0.03)	(0.10)	(−0.30)
Priv credit*$shock_{t-2}$	26.09	40.46	2.85	38.12	−1.2544	−1.2025	−1.1847	−1.5159
	(1.46)	(2.06)**	(0.14)	(2.08)**	(−2.12)**	(−2.04)**	(−2.75)***	(−2.45)**

Controls								
Linear trend	Yes	Yes	Yes	Yes	Yes	Yes	Yes	Yes
Intell rights + interact	Yes	Yes	Yes			Yes	Yes	
Prop rights + interact		Yes	Yes				Yes	
R^2 within	0.2535	0.2581	0.2295	0.2848	0.5053	0.5804	0.6228	0.5084
R^2 between	0.0519	0.1470	0.1016	0.0635	0.2292	0.1518	0.2325	0.2227
# countries (groups)	14	14	13	14	14	14	13	14
N	337	291	221	331	338	291	221	332

Note: Dependent variable is investment as a share of GDP or R&D as a share of investment. Annual 1973–97 data, except where lost due to lags. Panel fixed effects estimation. Shockt, shockt-1, shockt-2 refer to the contemporaneous, 1-year and 2-year lagged commodity price shock, as defined in the text. Lagged (t-10,t-6) or (t-5,t-1) average used for private credit, as indicated in the column heading. All regressions include a constant term and a linear trend. T-statistics in parenthesis. ***, **, * significant at the 1%, 5%, and 10% respectively.

Source: AABM (2004), table 7.

also be positive. We are particularly interested by the interaction term $\alpha_4 \cdot \text{shock}_{it} * \text{priv}_{it}$ and we predict that α_4 should be negative, which says that a higher level of financial development will imply a lower sensitivity of growth to shocks. In the estimation we allow for country-specific fixed effects.

Table 2.2 summarizes the results from AABM. In particular, it shows evidence of a significantly positive effect of shocks on medium-run growth. We also observe a strong negative coefficient on the interaction term, although it is only significant when we consider changes in the terms of trade. This result is shown to be robust to alternative measures of financial development and to using a one-period lagged value of private credit. Because of the substantial time-series variation in private credit it is not surprising that using its initial 1960 value produces an insignificant interaction term.

The final link that remains to be established is the interaction of financial development with the cyclicality of long-term investment and total investment with respect to exogenous shocks. As a proxy for long-term investment, AABM use data on R&D expenditures. Using annual data on 14 OECD countries between 1973 and 1997, AABM perform two first-stage regressions, respectively for R&D as a share of total investment ($\text{R\&D}_{it}/I_{it}$) and investment as a fraction of GDP (I_{it}/GDP_{it}) for country i in year t, as a function of current and lagged shocks and current and lagged shocks (one and two period lags) interacted with private credit in the country during subperiod t. As before, they include a linear trend and allow for country fixed effects.

Table 2.3 displays the results from these two regressions. Column (5) uses the moving average of private credit over the immediately preceding 5 years. In line with the model, we see that positive shocks stimulate R&D for a given level of total investment, but the ratio of R&D over total investment tends to be countercyclical in the absence of credit constraints. In particular, all coefficients on lagged shocks are positive, while the interaction terms of these shocks with private credit have a negative and significant coefficient. Two-year lagged shocks are the only significant ones, suggesting that the reallocation of investment itself takes place with a lag. To gauge the importance of credit constraints, note that R&D is procyclical for low levels of financial development but a value for private credit of $0.74/1.25 = 60\%$ is enough to make long-term investment countercyclical with respect to twice-lagged shocks. In fact, we observe such high levels of loan availability for many countries in our sample of 70, with the number tripling to 36 between 1974 and 1999. These results are shown to be robust to using the 5-year lagged 5-year average of private credit (Columns (6)–(8)).

In contrast to the above findings, the share of total investment in GDP does not become more procyclical as credit constraints tighten (Table 2.3, Columns (1)–(4)). If anything, financial development may magnify the procyclicality of the investment over GDP ratio, if we rely on the only significant (and positive) interaction coefficients in Columns (2) and (4). Overall, these results support our theory that credit availability redirects resources toward long-term projects (such as R&D) during a downturn, translating into improved growth a year or two later.

2.3 Toward a macropolicy of growth

In this chapter, we have proposed an explanation for the observed negative correlation between volatility and growth across countries, and also for the fact that the correlation is more significantly negative once we include non-OECD countries in the regressions. Our explanation combines credit constraints with entrepreneurs' choice between short-term capital and long-term growth-enhancing (R&D) investments. The main predictions from the theory are that in economies with lower levels of financial development: (i) volatility affects growth more negatively; (ii) growth is more sensitive to trade or price commodity shocks; (iii) R&D is more procyclical. As argued in the previous section and in greater detail in AABM, all these predictions are validated by available cross-country panel data on volatility, growth, R&D, and total investments over the period 1960–95.

To conclude this chapter, we would like to suggest two directions in which to pursue this research program and exploit our main findings so far. Both avenues have to do with the interplay between macropolicy and long-run growth, a topic on which endogenous growth theory has so far remained relatively silent.[3] The first avenue, currently explored by Aghion–Bacchetta–Ranciere–Rogoff (2004), henceforth ABRR, concerns the relationship between long-run growth and the choice of exchange rate regime. The second avenue, currently explored by Aghion-Barro–Marinescu, henceforth ABM, builds on the analysis in this chapter to revisit budgetary policies and their effects on long-run growth.

2.3.1 *Productivity growth and the choice of exchange rate regime*

The existing theoretical literature on exchange rates and open macroeconomics does not look at long-run growth, except for few regressions (e.g., by Ghosh *et al.* 2003) that did not find any systematic relationship between the two. Based on a variant of the model in this chapter, but with nominal rigidities so that nominal exchange rates can have an impact on real decisions and outcomes, ABRR predict that in economies with lower level of financial development, a flexible exchange rate regime will tend to generate excessive currency appreciations which in turn will make all firms (including the best performing ones) become more vulnerable to other shocks, for example, on the liquidity needs of long-term (productivity-enhancing) investments. This, in turn, will tend to discourage innovative investments.

ABRR consider a growing, small open economy with overlapping generations of entrepreneurs and workers. They assume that nominal wages are rigid and that the central bank either fixes the nominal exchange rate or follows an interest rate rule. The model focuses on the interaction of nominal exchange rate fluctuations and productivity growth.

The small open economy produces a single good identical to the world good. At each period a new generation of two-period lived individuals is born. One half of the individuals is selected to become entrepreneurs, while the other half become workers. If entrepreneurs go bankrupt when young, they become workers when old and are replaced by old workers in the firm. Since we abstract from saving and capital accumulation, individuals consume their income each period.

---

[3] A notable exception is the work by King *et al.* (1988) based on the AK approach.

During the first period of their life, entrepreneurs can produce using a technology with current average productivity, namely:

$$y_t = A_t \, (l_t)^\alpha \,,$$

where $\alpha < 1$ and l_t is labor input. At the end of the first period, entrepreneurs can invest in innovation and thereby realize extra rents in their second period. The foreign price of the good is taken as given. Purchasing power parity (PPP) holds so that

$$P_t = S_t P_t^*,$$

where P_t is the domestic price level and S_t is the nominal exchange rate (domestic per foreign currency). In a fixed exchange rate, one would set $S_t = \bar{S}$, while under a flexible exchange rate one has $E(S_t) = \bar{S}$. The nominal wage is preset before knowing nominal shocks, but after productivity is known, and it is preset at a level equal to the reservation wage of workers.

The entrepreneur chooses l_t to maximize *ex ante* expected profits, which in turn yields an equilibrium expected profit of the form:

$$\Pi_t = \kappa \cdot S_t^{1/(1-\alpha)}, \tag{2.2}$$

where κ is a constant (see ABRR for details). Thus, more volatile exchange rates translate into more volatile current profits.

Next, ABRR introduce innovation and credit constraints. As in AABM, they assume that an entrepreneur can remain active in the second period of his/her life, and thereby upgrade his/her technology, provided he/she can pay a liquidity cost (or "innovation cost") c^i, which in principle differs across firms and must be incurred by each firm at the end of its first period. We assume that the net productivity gain from innovating is sufficiently high that it is profitable for any entrepreneur to invest in innovation.

Again, in order to pay for the liquidity cost, the entrepreneur can borrow on the local credit market. However, we assume the existence of credit constraints which prevents him/her from borrowing more than a finite multiple $\mu \Pi_t$ of his/her current profits. We take μ as the measure of financial development.

Thus, the funds available for innovative investment at the end of the first period, are at most equal to $(1 + \mu)\Pi_t$ and therefore the entrepreneur will continue in the second period of his/her life whenever:

$$(1 + \mu)\Pi_t \geq c^i. \tag{2.3}$$

Using (2.2), this gives:

$$S_t^{1/(1-\alpha)} \geq \frac{c^i}{(1 + \mu)\kappa}, \tag{2.4}$$

or by taking logs:

$$s_t \geq (1 - \alpha)\ln\frac{c^i}{(1 + \mu)\kappa}, \tag{2.5}$$

where $s_t = \ln S_t$.

Thus, an entrepreneur is more likely to continue when the exchange rate is depreciated and with a large level of financial development. We now turn to the determination of the exchange rate.

ABRR follow AABM in assuming that knowledge A_t grows at a rate which is proportional to the total number of innovations in the economy, and for notational simplicity let us assume that it is equal to that number. By the law of large numbers the rate of productivity growth is thus simply equal to:

$$g_t = \Pr\left(s_t \geq (1 - \alpha)\ln\left(\frac{c^i}{(1 + \mu)\kappa}\right)\right).$$

We can now analyze how the average growth rate depends upon the variance of s_t, the level of financial development μ, and the interaction between the two. For example, if $c^i = 1$ for all firms and the exchange rate s_t is uniformly distributed on the interval $[-\varepsilon, \varepsilon]$, so that exchange rate volatility is then measured by ε, the expected growth rate at date t is simply equal to:

$$G_t(a_t, \mu) = \frac{1}{2} + \frac{(1 - \alpha)\ln[(1 + \mu)\kappa]}{2\varepsilon}.$$

Differentiating the above expression yields our main theoretical predictions: The average growth rate decreases with exchange rate volatility, and this effect is stronger with a lower *level of financial development as measured by* μ.

In economies with high levels of financial development, exchange rate flexibility may enhance average growth by weeding out the less innovative firms while promoting the more innovative. One should thus expect exchange rate flexibility to be more damaging to long-run growth when the degree of financial development is lower. This prediction turns out to be fully vindicated by the data. In particular, using a GMM panel data system estimator for 83 countries over a sequence of 5-year subperiods between 1961 and 2000, ABRR regress the growth rate of output per worker on exchange rate flexibility (computed from the same classification as in Rogoff *et al.* (2003)) and its interaction with financial development. The results are summarized in Table 2.4. We see that the direct effect of exchange rate flexibility on growth is negative and significant, while the interaction term between financial development and exchange rate flexibility has a positve and significant coefficient. Thus, as predicted by the model above, the higher the degree of financial development, the less negative the effect of exchange rate flexibility on growth.

This result may have interesting policy implications. For example, it may raise further questions for those European countries that are contemplating joining the EMU system. Given their level of financial development, should they tie their hands by adopting the Euro rather than maintaining a fully flexible exchange rate regime? The above result may also call for further organizational changes within the Euro zone, so that it would look more like one country with a flexible exchange rate *vis-à-vis* the rest of the world.

2.3.2 *Productivity growth and countercyclical budgetary policy*

A second avenue for policy analysis also based on the basic insights of AABM, and currently explored by ABM, is to analyze budgetary policies over the business cycle and their effects on long-run growth. The above analysis showed that in countries with lower financial development, negative shocks or higher volatility have more damaging effects on mean R&D investment and growth. This, in turn, may suggest that countercyclical budgetary policies should be more growth-enhancing in countries with lower degrees of financial development.

For example, consider the following cross-country panel regression involving 19 OECD countries over the period 1961–2000, divided in 10-year subperiods. Budgetary policies are captured

Table 2.4 Regression of growth rate of output per worker on exchange rate flexibility

Period:	1961–2000			
Unit of observation:	Non-overlapping 5-year averages System GMM			
Estimation technique:	[1]	[2]	[3]	[4]
Degree of Exchange Flexibility	−0.1890*	−0.4405**	−1.1613**	−0.7847**
(Rogoff *et al.* classification)	0.1107	0.1728	0.3144	0.3392
Financial Development	0.8449**	0.5420**	0.7368**	0.7108**
(private domestic credit/GDP, in logs)	0.1292	0.2063	0.1903	0.2207
Distance to Frontier	0.0085	−0.0424	0.7947**	0.7108**
(log(Initial Output per worker US/Initial Output per worker))	0.0870	0.1136	0.1427	0.2207
Flexibility*Financial Development		0.1007**		0.0976*
		0.0504		0.0537
Flexibility*Distance to Frontier			−0.5314**	−0.4844**
			0.1018	0.1135
Control variables				
Education	0.8327**	0.5420**	0.8052**	0.8617**
(secondary enrollment, in logs)	0.1487	0.2063	0.1679	0.1778
Trade Openness	0.5471**	0.6931**	0.9036**	1.0193**
(structure-adjusted trade volume/GDP, in logs)	0.2162	0.2552	0.3177	0.3399
Government Burden	−1.6837**	−0.4405**	−1.8885**	−1.7992**
(government consumption/GDP, in logs)	0.2032	0.1728	0.2235	0.2766
Lack of Price Stability	−4.0660**	−4.1598**	−3.5742**	−3.5272**
(inflation rate, in log [100+inf. rate])	0.4689	0.4792	0.4819	0.5535
Intercept	21.4569**	22.7512**	18.1347**	18.5464**
	2.631951	2.8698	2.8700	3.5767

Note: Dependent Variable: Growth Rate of Output per Worker (Standard errors are presented below the corresponding coefficient). **, * significant at the 5% and 10% respectively.

Table 2.5 Measure of countercyclicality of budgetary policies

Period: 1961–2000, divided into four 10-year periods	
Distance to Frontier	−14.4913**
	1.7072
Education	0.2222
	0.1730
Budgetary Activism	1.7784**
(std. dev. of primary deficit over std. dev. of output gap[1])	0.7153
Countercyclicality	0.7336*
(correlation of primary budget deficit and output gap)	0.4179
Budgetary Activism*Financial Development	−0.0181**
	0.0073
Countercyclicality*Financial Development	−0.0106**
	0.0044
Intercept	8.3357**
	1.8130

Note: Dependent Variable: Growth Rate of Productivity (Standard errors are presented below the corresponding coefficient). **, * significant at the 5% and 10% respectively.
[1] The output gap is measured as potential output minus actual output. Thus, a positive correlation implies countercyclical budgetary policy.

by two alternative measures. First, as a measure of budgetary activism, ABM use the ratio between the standard deviation of the primary deficit and the standard deviation of the output gap over a 10-year period. Second, ABM construct a measure of countercyclicality of budgetary policies by taking the average correlation between the primary deficit and the output gap over a 10-year period.[4] One can regress productivity growth on these two variables and their interactions with financial development. The regression in Table 2.5 shows both, a positive and significant direct effect of budgetary activism on productivity growth, and positive and significant direct effect of countercyclicality of budgetary policy on productivity growth. More importantly, the interaction

[4] Here, the output gap is measured as potential GDP minus actual GDP, implying that a positive correlation between the primary deficit and the output gap stands for countercyclical budgetary policy.

terms of both variables with financial development have negative and significant coefficients, which confirms the prediction that
less financially developed economies should benefit more from
countercyclical fiscal policies.

ABM intend to go further by performing two-stage regression procedures in which: (i) the first stage regresses government
primary deficits for each country on the current output gap, the
current departure from trend government expenditures, and debt
repayments, under the assumption that governments pursue some
kind of a tax smoothing objective (see Barro (1986) for theoretical
foundations underlying such a first-stage specification); (ii) the
second stage regresses average growth over a given period on financial development, the degree of countercyclicality of budgetary
policy as it comes out of the first-stage regression for each country, and the interaction between financial development and the
countercyclicality coefficient. This coefficient in turn replaces the
previous two measures of activism and countercyclicality, now
assuming that governments follow a prespecified objective. Pre-
liminary results confirm the findings in Table 2.5, namely that
countercyclical budgetary policies are more growth-enhancing
when the level of financial development is lower. Interestingly,
the European Union is less financially developed than the United
States, and yet it advocates and also implements budgetary
policies that are far less countercyclical than in the United States.
Is that one among several potential explanations for the European
stagnation *vis-à-vis* the United States?

3

Endogeneizing Volatility: Pecuniary Externalities and the Credit Channel

In the previous chapters we have focused on the effects of aggregate volatility and aggregate productivity or trade shocks on long-run growth, taking volatility as being largely exogenous. In this and the following chapters we show how volatility can emerge endogenously, in a world where credit constraints sometimes bind.

Until recently, the dominant paradigm to explain persistent macroeconomic volatility in market economies has been the so-called Real Business Cycles model pioneered by Kydland and Prescott (1982) and by Long and Plosser (1987). In its simplest version, the model is based on three elements. First, the dynamics of productivity, of the form:

$$\ln A_t = \rho \ln A_{t-1} + \varepsilon_t,$$

where ε_t is a random noise (independently and identically distributed over time) whose variance measures the magnitude of the productivity shocks and ρ is a parameter that measures the persistence of the shocks over time. Second, the production technology

$$Y_t = A_t F(K_t, L_t),$$

where F exhibits constant returns to scale with respect to capital (K_t) and labor (L_t). The first two equations describe the demand side of the labor market. The supply side is pinned down by a third element, namely the representative individual's utility for consumption and leisure

$$U(c_t, L_t) = \ln c_t - \frac{\theta}{1 - \eta} \left(L_t^{1-\eta} - 1 \right),$$

where η measures the elasticity of labor supply.

This model provides a very simple explanation for why even small productivity shocks can induce large and persistent output fluctuations: suppose the occurrence of a positive productivity shock. This will increase the relative attractiveness of work relative to leisure, and all the more so when the elasticity of labor supply η is sufficiently close to 1. This in turn will amplify the positive effect of the productivity shock on the equilibrium output Y_t.

There are several problems with this approach. First, for small technological shocks to generate large and persistent fluctuations in aggregate GDP and employment, one needs to assume very large values for the variance of ε_t and a persistence parameter ρ very close to 1.[1] Second, to account for the fact that large fluctuations in employment occur in practice with little change in real wage, one needs to assume a labor supply elasticity parameter η also very close to 1. But then, how can we explain that volatility has been so much higher in Asia or Latin America over the past three decades when the elasticity of labor supply is higher in the United States? Table 3.1 gives estimates of the income-compensated wage elasticities of labor supply for several Asian countries, Peru, and the United States. The elasticity is highest in the United States, with a value of 0.11. Third, there seem to be many more recessions than large negative shocks that could explain them: There is the example of the negative trade shock that occurred in Finland upon the collapse of the Soviet Union in 1991, but it is hard to find large negative productivity shocks after 1975 in Latin America or in Asia. For all of these reasons, the literature on explaining

Table 3.1 Income-compensated
wage elasticity of labour supply

Taiwan	−0.12
Malaysia	−0.07
Korea(South)	0
Thailand	0.08
Peru	0.1
US Average	0.11

[1] These parameter restrictions can be relaxed to some extent, for example, by introducing intersectoral rigidities as in Long and Plosser (1983) or increasing returns and large industry fixed costs as in Hall (1991). However, fixed costs are not that high in the IT or service sectors which are becoming increasingly prominent in developed economies. An alternative way to increase the effects of exogenous productivity shocks on aggregate output fluctuations, is to introduce price stickiness or imperfect competition and menu costs.

macroeconomic volatility have come to the conclusion that credit constraints probably do have a role to play in this story.

The basic intuition for why credit constraints may contribute to volatility is laid out in an important paper by Bernanke–Gertler (1989), henceforth BG, and Bernanke *et al.* (1998). These papers explore the effects of the so-called "financial accelerator" whereby the existence of credit constraints limits firms' investment to a finite multiple of their current cash flow (as in our model earlier). This financial accelerator in turns amplifies the effects of real and nominal shocks. In particular, small changes in real interest rates induced by monetary policy, or small changes in the cost structure of firms resulting from a productivity shock, can have large real effects as they affect firms' investment capacity. This in turn will have a negative impact on cash flows in subsequent periods, thereby propagating and amplifying the initial shock over time. To show evidence of a financial accelerator, Bernanke *et al.* use the Quarterly Financial Report for Manufacturing, Mining, and Trade Corporations published by the US Department of Commerce, which contains quarterly time-series information for small and large US firms. They show that small manufacturing firms (which are typically more credit constrained than large firms[2]) experience more procyclical variations in sales, inventories, and short-term debt than larger firms, which they take as evidence of the existence of a financial accelerator. The BG model is a partial equilibrium model, where interest rates changes are exogenous. Moreover, what credit constraints do in their model is to amplify shocks: There is not yet a theory of persistent business cycles.

Kiyotaki and Moore (1997), henceforth KM, show a way of extending the BG insight into a theory of persistent business cycles. In their model, a positive shock to profits raises investment which, in turn, increases the price of collateral. This in turn relaxes borrowing constraints on investors and therefore improves their investment capacity. This in turn amplifies the positive shock on profits. Hence, the possibility of positive serial correlation in aggregate output over time. KM also show that this general equilibrium effect via the price of collateral can generate persistent fluctuations, that is negative serial correlation in aggregate output,

---

[2] In particular, the short-term debt of small firms consists almost exclusively of bank loans, whereas the short-term debt of large firms includes bank loans and commercial paper.

in an extended version of their models with lags in the response of investment to changes in borrowing constraints. However, they offer no simple intuition for why the positive serial correlation underlying their basic amplification mechanism suddenly turns into a negative serial correlation and relatedly, the model does not give us much insight into the conditions under which endogenous cycles are most likely to occur. Finally, neither BG nor KM lay out the long-run growth implications of the amplification or endogenous volatility phenomena described in these papers.

In this and the next chapter, we develop an elementary theoretical framework which generates endogenous and persistent volatility in a growing economy with credit constraints. The basic mechanism is the interaction of credit constraints and endogenous changes in market prices. We begin with a version that is relevant for a closed economy, where the important market price is the interest rate. In the next chapter, we present an alternative version built around a small open economy, and argue that a similar mechanism operates there, even though the interest rate is fixed by the world capital markets. This is because there are endogenous movements in the real exchange rate. We argue that the model can account for a number of observed facts about lending booms and crises in emerging market economies. It also provides additional arguments in favor of countercyclical budgetary policies in less financially developed economies. The remaining part of this chapter is organized as follows. Section 3.1 outlines a simple AK growth model with credit constraints and pecuniary externalities among investors. Section 3.2 defines booms and slumps in the context of the model, and Section 3.3 analyzes the dynamics of the model. Section 3.4 derives sufficient conditions for the existence of a limit cycle and considers the long-run effects of exogenous shocks. Section 3.5 discusses the empirical relevance of the model. Section 3.6 turns the attention to policy analysis and the effects of countercyclical budgetary policies.

3.1 A simple framework

We consider an economy where growth is driven by capital accumulation, although the main argument could easily be adapted to the case of a knowledge-based economy where growth is primarily driven by (long-term) innovative investments. Time is discrete and indexed by t. Labor is supplied inelastically and $L_0 = 1$ is the aggregate labor supply. There is one good in the economy, which is used both for consumption and also as capital input, and is produced according to the standard AK technology:

$$Y = AK^\beta L^{1-\beta} K_a^\gamma,$$

where K_a is the aggregate capital stock and

$$\gamma = 1 - \beta.$$

As in the neoclassical model or the AK model with constant savings rate,[3] we assume that all agents consume a fixed fraction α of current period's earnings and save the fixed fraction $(1 - \alpha)$ for investment or lending in the next period.

Using the fact that all firms are identical, we focus on the symmetric equilibrium where they all invest the same amount of capital each period. Then, in equilibrium:

$$Y_t = \sigma K_t,$$

where

$$\sigma = AL_0^{1-\beta} = A.$$

Moreover, the capital share of output is equal to $\beta Y_t = \beta \sigma K_t = \sigma_1 K$, whereas the labor share of output is equal to $(1 - \beta)Y_t = (1 - \beta)\sigma K_t$.

Only firm owners (the capitalists) have access to productive investment opportunities. Workers cannot invest directly in production but they can either lend at the current interest rate r to the borrowers (or entrepreneurs), or invest in a home activity that yields a (low) return rate

$$\sigma_2 < \sigma_1 = \beta\sigma.$$

---

[3] See Frankel (1962).

The two key elements of the story we tell in this chapter are *credit constraints* and *price effects*.

1. Credit constraints are modeled as in the previous chapter, by assuming that an entrepreneur with initial wealth W can invest at most μW in the current period. This means that a firm that has a cash flow shock will respond by changing its investment.

2. Price effects work through the interest rate which is determined endogenously. The AK nature of the model implies that the equilibrium interest rate will be equal to the rate of return σ_1 on capital investment whenever investment demand is higher than aggregate savings, and will drop down to σ_2 when investment demand is less than aggregate savings. This in turn affects the ability of the firm to borrow, which affects investment demand, and so on.

The timing of events within each period t is depicted in Figure 3.1.

Borrowing and lending take place at the beginning of the period (which we denote by t^-) at an interest rate which is determined as specified above, by the comparison between investment demand and aggregate savings. And everything else happens at the end of the period (which we denote by t^+), namely: the realization of returns from investments, the repayment of debt from borrowers to lenders, and finally consumption and savings decisions which in turn determine the total amount of savings available at the beginning of the following period $(t + 1)^-$.

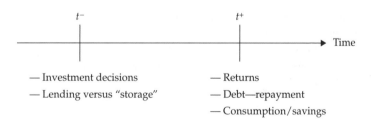

FIG. 3.1 Timing.
Source: Aghion *et al.* (1999a), figure 1.

3.2 *Booms and slumps*

Let W_B^t and W_L^t denote the wealth of entrepreneurs and workers at the beginning of period $(t+1)$. Total savings from the previous period t is by definition equal to:

$$S_t = W_B^t + W_L^t.$$

Total investment demand in the (high-yield) production activity by entrepreneurs, is equal to:

$$I_{t+1}^d = \mu W_B^t.$$

From our discussion in the previous section, the equilibrium interest rate r_{t+1} in period $(t+1)$ is equal to $\sigma_1 = \beta\sigma$ if $I_{t+1}^d > S_t$ and it is equal to σ_2 otherwise.

Moreover, in this AK model, the rate of return on the high-yield production technology remains equal to σ_1 at all levels of investment. Thus entrepreneurs who always seek to maximize their end-of-period wealth (which allows them to maximize consumption and savings), will try to invest up to their investment capacity $\mu W_B^t = I_{t+1}^d$, and will only fail to achieve that goal if the total amount of savings is lower than their investment demand. Actual investment in the high-yield production activity at date $(t+1)$ will thus be equal to:

$$\min\left(S_t, I_{t+1}^d\right).$$

Consequently, investment in the low-yield (home) activity will be equal to the residual

$$S_t - \min\left(S_t, I_{t+1}^d\right),$$

and in particular it will be positive only due to the limited borrowing capacity of entrepreneurs. In the absence of credit constraints, entrepreneurs would always be able to absorb the total amount of savings and thereby maximize their end-of-period revenues.

During periods when investment demand is higher than aggregate savings, all savings are invested in the high-yield production activity, so that the growth rate of the economy is the AK (or Harrod–Domar) rate, defined as the ratio between output in two successive periods[4]:

$$\overline{g} = (1 - \alpha)\sigma.$$

We refer to these periods as "booms." In contrast, during periods when investment demand is less than aggregate savings, the fraction,

$$\frac{S_t - \min\left(S_t, I_{t+1}^d\right)}{S_t} = 1 - \frac{I_{t+1}^d}{S_t} = 1 - f_t,$$

of aggregate savings is invested in the low-yield activity at rate σ_2 so that the growth rate is lower than $\overline{g}$, equal to:

$$g_t = f_t^{\cdot}\sigma + (1 - f_t)\sigma_2 < \overline{g}.$$

We refer to such periods as "slumps."

3.3 Dynamic equations

Using the fact that actual borrowing by entrepreneurs, that must be repaid at interest rate r_{t+1}, is equal to the difference between actual investment and their initial wealth W_B^t, we can proceed to describing the dynamic evolution of the economy. This dynamics is fully described by the state variables W_B^t and W_L^t, and as we will now show, it boils down to a single dynamic equation in the one state variable

$$q^t = \frac{S_t}{I_{t+1}^d} = \frac{1}{f_t}.$$

Consider first the dynamic evolution of wealth during a boom. If period $(t + 1)$ is a boom, we know that investment demand at $(t + 1)^-$ is higher than aggregate savings (that is, $I_{t+1}^d > S_t$), so actual investment in the high-yield activity is equal to $S_t = W_B^t + W_L^t$ and the equilibrium interest rate is high, equal to σ_1. It then follows that the dynamics of (borrowing) entrepreneurs'

---

[4] This growth rate is also equal to the product of the savings rate $(1 - \alpha)$ and of the output/capital ratio σ.

wealth W_B and (lending) workers' wealth W_L between periods $(t+1)$ and $(t+2)$, are given by:

$$W_B^{t+1} = (1-\alpha)\left[\beta\sigma(W_B^t + W_L^t) - \sigma_1 W_L^t\right],$$
$$W_L^{t+1} = (1-\alpha)\left[(1-\beta)\sigma(W_B^t + W_L^t) + \sigma_1 W_L^t\right]. \tag{B}$$

In other words, given that available savings $(W_B^t + W_L^t)$ are invested in the high-yield production activity during a boom, total revenue from this activity is equal to $\sigma(W_B^t + W_L^t)$. A fraction β of that revenue remunerates entrepreneurs but they must repay the high interest rate σ_1 to the lenders on the amount W_L^t they have borrowed from them,[5] hence the term $(-\sigma_1 W_L^t)$ on the right-hand side of the first equation, which mirrors the term $\sigma_1 W_L^t$ on the right-hand side of the second equation. Finally a fraction $(1-\beta)$ of the production revenue must remunerate labor as wage payments.

Consider now the dynamic evolution of wealth during a recession. If period $(t+1)$ is a recession, investment demand at $(t+1)^-$ is lower than aggregate savings (that is, $I_{t+1}^d < S_t$) so that actual investment in the high-yield activity is equal to $I_{t+1}^d = \mu W_B^t$ and the equilibrium interest rate is low, equal to σ_2. It then follows that the dynamics of W_B and W_L between $(t+1)$ and $(t+2)$, are given by:

$$W_B^{t+1} = (1-\alpha)\left[\beta\sigma\mu W_B^t - \sigma_2(\mu-1)W_B^t\right],$$
$$W_L^{t+1} = (1-\alpha)\left[(1-\beta)\sigma\mu W_B^t + \sigma_2 W_L^t\right]. \tag{S}$$

In other words, given that only the amount μW_B^t can be invested in the high-yield activity during a slump, this activity will generate a revenue equal to $\sigma\mu W_B^t$. A fraction β of that revenue remunerates entrepreneurs, who must now pay the low equilibrium interest rate σ_2 on their net borrowing $(\mu-1)W_B^t$, and a fraction $(1-\beta)$ of that same revenue must remunerate labor. In addition, workers

---

[5] Since

$$W_B^t + W_L^t < I_{t+1}^d = \mu W_B^t,$$

the actual amount borrowed by entrepreneurs in a boom, namely W_L^t, falls short of their net borrowing capacity

$$(\mu-1)W_B^t.$$

realize the rate of return σ_2 on their entire wealth W_L^t, both by lending a fraction of it (at rate σ_2) to entrepreneurs and by investing the remaining fraction on their home activity at the same rate.

Letting

$$q^t = \frac{S_t}{I_{t+1}^d} = \frac{1}{f_t},$$

denote the ratio of savings over investment demand, simple manipulations of the above systems of equation lead to

$$q^{t+1} = \frac{q^t}{\beta}, \tag{B$'$}$$

when $q^t \leq 1$ (i.e. when the economy is in a boom in period $t+1$) and

$$q^{t+1} = \frac{(\sigma - \sigma_2) + \sigma_2 q^t}{\mu(\beta\sigma - \sigma_2) + \sigma_2}, \tag{S$'$}$$

when $q^t > 1$ (i.e. when the economy is in a slump in period $t + 1$). Equations (B$'$) and (S$'$) define a simple first-order difference equation which completely determines the dynamics of the economy.

3.4 Endogenous volatility and amplified shocks

The above dynamics can be easily analyzed graphically. In Figure 3.2, B and S denote the two lines corresponding to equations (B$'$) and (S$'$) respectively. Since $\beta < 1$, the B line lies above the 45° line which it intersects at $q^t = q^{t+1} = 0$, whereas the S line has a positive intersect since it has a slope strictly less than 1, so that it intersects the 45° line at

$$q^* = s = \frac{(\sigma - \sigma_2)(1/\mu)}{\beta\sigma - \sigma_2}.$$

At this point there are only two possibilities. Either $s > 1$, in which case the economy converges to a permanent slump, with

$$q^t \longrightarrow s > 1,$$

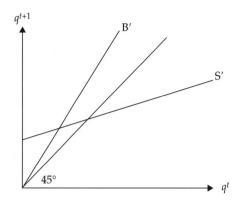

FIG. 3.2 Graphic depiction of equations (B′) and (S′).

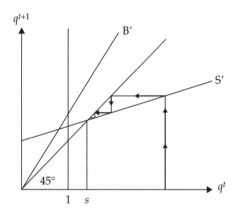

FIG. 3.3 The permanent slump regime.

so that indeed investment demand is always less than total savings for *t* sufficiently large. This case is depicted in Figure 3.3. Or *s* < 1, in which case the economy will converge to a limit cycle, as shown in Figure 3.4, oscillating between boom and slump phases.

The intuition for these cycles can be simply summarized as follows. Starting from a slump phase, investments and borrowing will resume growing over time as entrepreneurs are getting richer, and eventually, investment capacity μW_{B}^{t} will run ahead of savings. At this point, savings will be fully employed in the high-yield

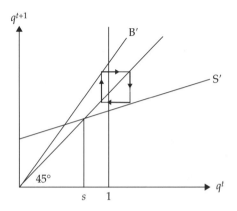

FIG. 3.4 The cycles regime.

technology which means that the economy will grow fast at rate $\bar{g}$, but the interest rate will also rise up to $\sigma_1 = \beta\sigma$. This rise in interest rate will increase the debt burden of all entrepreneurs (this is the pecuniary externality part of the story). The rise in the debt burden will slow down the growth of entrepreneurs' wealth and therefore that of their investment capacity (this is the credit constraint part of the story) relative to that of total savings, so that at some point investment capacity will fall below total savings, at which point the economy will enter a slump phase and the interest rate will fall to σ_2. The economy will then grow at a rate lower than $\bar{g}$, however, the low interest rate will allow entrepreneurs to rebuild their investment capacity so as to eventually absorb all aggregate savings, at this point the economy will reenter a boom, and so on.

Two remarks are worth making at this point:

1. Note that the economy may stay for several periods in a row in one regime (either boom or slump) before switching to the other regime, as shown in Figures 3.5 and 3.6.

2. Persistent limit cycles occur when

$$s < 1,$$

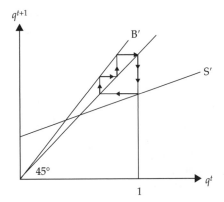

FIG. 3.5 Prolonged boom (debt buildup).

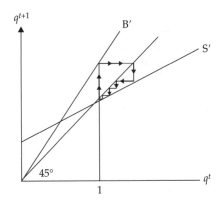

FIG. 3.6 Prolonged recession (profit reconstitution).

or equivalently when

$$\mu > \frac{\sigma - \sigma_2}{\beta\sigma - \sigma_2},$$

that is for sufficiently high levels of financial development as measured by the credit multiplier μ. In particular, a highly underdeveloped economy in which entrepreneurs rely entirely on their retained earnings for investment (that is, where $\mu = 1$) will not cycle. On the other hand, an economy

where firms face no credit constraint and can invest up to
the expected net present value of their projects, will not
experience long-term volatility either, as

$$q^t \longrightarrow 0 < 1,$$

in that case. It is thus only those economies at intermediate
levels of financial development which will experience persistent fluctuations. Thus, the model provides an explanation
for why we tend to observe more volatility in middle-income
countries in Asia or Latin America than either in highly
developed countries like the United States or the highly
underdeveloped countries of Africa.

Finally, let us analyze what exogenous productivity shocks do
in this model, keeping in mind the usual criticism of the RBC
literature that it is unable to explain the magnitude of observed
fluctuations. More specifically, consider the effect of a temporary
shock that increases the productivity parameter σ, and suppose
that prior to this shock the economy is at the steady-state $q^t = s$.

From equation (S'), we immediately see that the positive shock
on σ shifts the S curve as shown in Figure 3.7, toward a modified

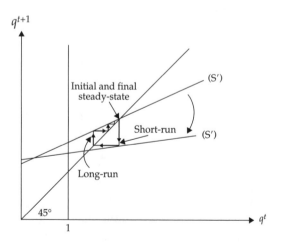

FIG. 3.7 Effect of temporary increase in σ.
Source: Aghion *et al.* (1999a), figure IXa.

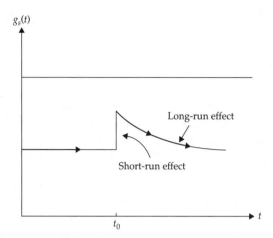

FIG. 3.8 Effect of temporary increase in σ on growth.
Source: Aghion *et al.* (1999a), figure IXb.

curve with lower slope and higher intercept. As a result, q^t falls before moving back up monotonically toward its initial value.

The growth rate equal to

$$g_t = \frac{1}{q_t}\sigma + \left(1 - \frac{1}{q_t}\right)\sigma_2,$$

will then evolve as shown in Figure 3.8, first increasing sharply and then going back slowly to its initial level. We thus see that the direct effect of the productivity shock on the growth rate (direct effect of σ on g_t) is amplified by the indirect effect through q_t: namely, a positive productivity shock increases entrepreneurs' wealth and therefore their borrowing capacity. This in turn allows them to absorb a higher fraction of aggregate savings into their high-yield production technology, which itself operates at (temporarily) higher productivity. The persistence is due to the fact that entrepreneurs' borrowing capacity is positively affected not only in the short run, but also after productivity has returned to its initial level, as entrepreneurs can carry their wealth from one period to the next.[6]

---

[6] This amplifying mechanism is essentially that pointed out by BG, although here it is analyzed in the context of a fully dynamic general equilibrium model.

3.5 Some facts about volatility in the United States

Three main empirical predictions emerge from the model in this chapter, namely:

1. The ratio of debt-obligations to firms' cash flow should peak toward the end of a boom, and thus increase sharply during the transition from a boom to a slump;
2. The effective interest rate faced by the corporate sector is procyclical;
3. The interest rates spread (e.g. the interest rate differential between 10-year bonds and 3-month commercial paper) should also increase sharply during the transition from a boom to a recession. The reason is that at the end of booms, firms have accumulated high levels of (long-term) debt and therefore face a high risk of bankruptcy or default over any new (long-term) debt issued during this period compared to the long run. Hence, it becomes hard for them to obtain further long-term credit, all they can hope for is to obtain short-term credit. This, in turn implies that the relative demand for short-term credit will increase sharply toward the end of booms.

The above model is of a (large) closed economy. Therefore the United States is a natural place to look for supporting evidence. And as it turns out, these predictions appear to be borne out by the data, at least until the early 1990s. Figure 3.9 below shows the dynamic evolution of the debt/cash flow ratio over the period 1959–99. The vertical bars correspond to the lowest point of recessions, and one can see that, almost always, the debt/cash flow sharply increases either during the recession or right before. Figure 3.10 shows the evolution of the 10-year and 3-month interest rate spread over the same period, and again it appears that in most cases the spread sharply increases during a recession.[7] In fact, the above predictions fit the US data particularly well before the mid-1980s. From 1959 until 1983, high debt/cash flows and/or

---

[7] Similarly, Stock and Watson (1997) show that the spread between rates on unsecured commercial paper and the rate on (nondefaulting) treasury bills increases sharply toward the end of booms, and then decreases during slumps.

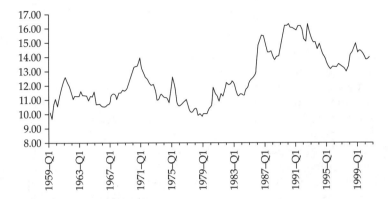

FIG. 3.9 Debt/cash flow ratio.

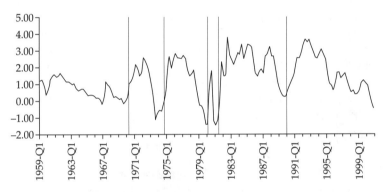

FIG. 3.10 10-year and 3-month spread.

high spreads are good predictors of a forthcoming recession, and the average interest rate incurred by firms is indeed highly procyclical, as shown by Friedman and Kuttner (1993). However, since the mid-1980s, macroeconomic volatility in the United States appears to be lower, recessions occur less often, and the correlation between credit indicators and recessions becomes much weaker. This might reflect the increasing financial sophistication of the US economy, which as in our model, insulates the economy from credit-driven cycles.

3.6 Policy implications

The model in this chapter has interesting policy implications as to what a government could do to limit the occurrence or length of recessions and thereby increase average growth over time. First, on a more structural front, generalizing the access to investment opportunities (or making workers become shareholders of firms) would make it more likely that aggregate savings be fully invested in the high-yield production activity. Similarly, allowing for foreign direct investment (i.e. for additional foreign wealth to be invested in new equity) would increase the borrowing capacity of investors as a whole, thereby again making it more likely that domestic savings be more fully invested in the high-yield production technology.

Second, for a given division of the economy between savers and investors, properly designed countercyclical transfer policies will also be growth-enhancing. More specifically, suppose that the economy is currently in a slump, so that the investment capacity of entrepreneurs μW_B^t is less than aggregate savings $S_t = W_B^t + W_L^t$ (i.e. $q^t > 1$). Then, in order to achieve the Harrod–Domar rate of growth $\bar{g}$, it suffices to redistribute wealth ΔW from savers to entrepreneurs, where

$$\mu\left(W_B^t + \Delta W\right) = W_B^t + W_L^t.$$

Such policy will ensure that all savings are invested in the high-yield production activity, so that indeed the growth rate of the economy is equal to

$$\bar{g} = (1 - \alpha)\sigma.$$

Note first that this redistribution policy need not hurt the savers: By raising investment capacity it also raises the demand for loanable funds and therefore the equilibrium interest rate from its depressed value σ_2 to its high value $\sigma_1 = \beta\sigma$. Thus, the interest income of savers moves from $\sigma_2 W_L^t$ to $\sigma_1\left(W_L^t - \Delta W\right)$ which is higher if the required wealth transfer ΔW is sufficiently small. This will be the case whenever the upcoming recession is not too severe. Moreover, if the wage rate has an efficiency wage component, so that employed workers earn positive rents, the wealth transfer

ΔW can benefit workers due to its expansionary effects on the labor market.

Next, the above type of transfers can be achieved through a standard countercyclical fiscal policy: since slumps are periods with idle savings, governments can promote recovery by issuing public debt in order to absorb those idle savings and thereby finance investment subsidies (or tax cuts) for businesses. More specifically, at the beginning of a recession period $t + 1$ (where therefore $q^t > 1$), the government should issue new public debt ΔB and use the proceeds to finance investment subsidies or tax cuts for entrepreneurs. The government must of course offer an interest rate on its new bonds which is at least equal to the rate of return on the low-yield home activity σ_2 in order for such bonds to be subscribed by savers. Public debt repayment at the end of the period is financed through tax revenues of an amount equal to $\Delta T = \sigma_2 \Delta B$ and raised on labor income or interest income. Such a countercyclical fiscal policy amounts to a direct transfer $\Delta W = \Delta B$ from savers to entrepreneurs. We thus obtain a new rationale for countercyclical budgetary policies, in addition to the one pointed out in the previous chapter.

4

Endogenous Volatility in an Open Economy

IN the previous chapter we argued that the interplay between credit constraints and the equilibrium interest rate acts as a propagation mechanism for exogenous shocks and in certain cases has the potential to generate persistent fluctuations. One way of getting rid of this particular problem is to open the economy (including the capital market), so that the interest rate no longer varies in response to demand conditions in the domestic economy.

However, we argue in this chapter that financial liberalization introduces a new problem: Now the real exchange rate, which is the relative price between nontradable and tradable goods, becomes a source of instability. It goes up in a boom, squeezing profits, which limits borrowing and hence investment and brings the economy down. The fact that the economy is open to capital inflows may actually make things worse, since it allows investment demand to grow very fast in a boom.

The chapter is organized as follows. Section 4.1 lays out the model. Section 4.2 describes the basic mechanism, characterizes the conditions under which macroeconomic volatility arises, and derives a first set of predictions. Section 4.3 shows that these predictions are consistent with the existing empirical literature on lending booms. Section 4.4 analyzes the impact of a capital account liberalization. Section 4.5 draws some policy conclusions.

4.1 A very simple model

For pedagogical purposes we consider a simple model with constant saving rates, a Leontief technology and a nontraded factor of production which is in fixed supply. Aghion *et al.* (2004a) sketch a more general version, which allows for an elastic supply of the nontraded factor, a CES production technology; and an endogenous saving rate.

Thus, consider a small open economy with a single tradable good produced with capital and a country-specific factor. One should typically think of this factor as input services such as (skilled) labor or real estate. We take the output good as the numeraire and denote by p the price of the country-specific factor when expressed in units of the output good. The relative price p can also be interpreted as the real exchange rate. In this basic framework we assume that the supply of the country-specific factor is inelastic and equal to Z.

As in the previous chapter, we assume that all agents *save* a fixed fraction $(1 - \alpha)$ of their total end-of-period wealth and thus consume a fixed fraction α.[1]

There are two distinct categories of individuals in the economy. First, the *lenders* who cannot directly invest in production, but can lend out their wealth at the fixed international market-clearing interest rate r. Second, there are the *entrepreneurs* (or *borrowers*) who are the people who have the opportunity to invest in production. There is a continuum of lenders and borrowers and their number is normalized to 1 for both categories.

Output y is given by the following production function:

$$y = \min\left(\frac{K}{a}, z\right), \tag{4.1}$$

where $(1/a) > r$, that is, we assume that productivity is larger than the world interest rate. K denotes the current level of capital and z denotes the level of the country-specific input. With perfect capital markets, investment would simply be determined by the international interest rate r.

Credit Market Imperfections: These are modeled as in the previous chapter, namely: an entrepreneur with initial wealth W_B can invest at most μW_B, whereas they would borrow up to the net present value of their project in the absence of credit constraints. As before the proportionality coefficient, or *credit multiplier* $\mu > 0$, reflects the level of financial development in the domestic economy, and an entrepreneur with initial wealth W_B at the beginning of the period, borrows $(\mu - 1)W_B = L$ if her credit constraint is binding.

---

[1] This assumption is relaxed in Aghion *et al.* (2004a). The intertemporal decisions of lenders are of no consequence for output in such an open economy since investors can borrow in international capital markets. They will, however, affect net capital flows.

The Timing of Events: The timing of events within each period t is the following. Investment, borrowing and lending, and the payment of the country-specific factor services $p \cdot z$ by entrepreneurs to the owners of that factor, take place at the *beginning* of the period (which we denote by t^-). Everything else occurs at the *end* of the period (which we denote by t^+): the returns to investments are realized; borrowers repay their debt, rL, to lenders; and finally, agents make their consumption and savings decisions determining in turn the initial wealth of borrowers at the beginning of the next period (i.e. at $(t + 1)^-$).

4.2 The dynamics

As in the previous chapter, we can treat the entrepreneurs' wealth W_B^t as the state variable. In fact, in an open economy the dynamics is simpler than in a closed economy in the sense that we do not need to keep track of domestic aggregate savings, and therefore of the wealth of domestic lenders. The reason is that loans come from both, domestic and foreign lenders and the total amount of loanable funds is therefore always greater than the investment capacity μW_B^t of domestic borrowers. Actual investment is thus always constrained by the wealth constraints of domestic firms, never by the supply of funds. We first derive the dynamic equations that describe the evolution of entrepreneurs' wealth over time. We then show under which conditions the open economy converges to a limit cycle.

4.2.1 Dynamic equations

Let W_B^{t+1} denote the disposable wealth of entrepreneurs (borrowers) at the beginning of period $t + 1$. The dynamic evolution of W_B (and therefore of investment and total output) between two successive periods is simply described by the equation:

$$W_B^{t+1} = (1 - \alpha)\left[e + y^t - r(\mu - 1)W_B^t\right], \qquad (4.2)$$

where e is some endowment income that entrepreneurs get in every period (measured in units of final output), $y^t = \min(K/a, Z)$

is output in period t (also equal to the gross revenues of entrepreneurs during that period). The expression in brackets is the *net* end-of-period t revenue of entrepreneurs. The net disposable wealth of entrepreneurs at the beginning of period $t + 1$ is what remains of this net end-of-period return after consumption, hence the multiplying factor $(1 - \alpha)$ on the right-hand side of equation (4.2).

Entrepreneurs invest and borrow only if their profits are larger than or equal to the international return. When μ or W_B are large, entrepreneurs invest only up to the point where $y - rL = rW_B$, where L denotes the amount of borrowings. Any remaining wealth is invested at the international market rate. In this case, no pure profits are earned from production and the evolution of wealth is simply given by:

$$W_B^{t+1} = (1 - \alpha) \left[e + rW_B^t \right]. \tag{4.3}$$

Thus, the dynamics are fully described either by difference equation (4.2) or by difference equation (4.3) and we now proceed to analyze under which conditions this dynamic system generates persistent endogenous fluctuations.

4.2.2 Two main effects of current wealth on future wealth

Let $I^t = \mu W_B^t$ denote the borrowing (or investment) capacity of domestic entrepreneurs at the beginning of period $t + 1$. Entrepreneurs will choose the level of the country-specific factor z, with corresponding investment $K^t = I^t - p^t \cdot z$, to maximize current profits, where p^t still denotes the current price of the nontradable (or country-specific) good in terms of the tradable. Given the above Leontief technology, the optimum involves

$$y^t = \frac{I^t - p^t \cdot z}{a} = z, \tag{4.4}$$

which in turn yields

$$y^t = \frac{I^t}{a + p^t} = \frac{\mu W_B^t}{a + p^t}.$$

The dynamic equation (4.2) can thus be rewritten:

$$W_B^{t+1} = (1 - \alpha) \left[e + \frac{\mu W_B^t}{a + p^t} - r(\mu - 1) W_B^t \right].$$

Now taking the derivative of W_B^{t+1} with respect to W_B^t, we obtain[2]:

$$\frac{dW_B^{t+1}}{dW_B^t} = (1 - \alpha) \left[\frac{\mu}{a + p^t} - r(\mu - 1) - \frac{y^t}{a + p^t} \frac{\partial p^t}{\partial W_B^t} \right], \qquad (4.5)$$

which in turn reveals two opposite effects of current wealth on future wealth.

1. A wealth effect. This effect corresponds to the term $(\mu / (a + p^t)) - r(\mu - 1))$ on the right-hand side of (4.3). In other words: for given price of the nontradable good, a higher level of current wealth W_B^t leads to higher output, which in turn improves the creditworthiness of entrepreneurs and thereby generates greater investment demand over the next period. This effect generates investment booms and a positive effect of current wealth on future wealth.

2. A price effect. This effect is captured by the term $y^t / (a + p^t) \times \partial p^t / \partial W_B^t$ on the right-hand side of (4.3). In other words, higher wealth in this period increases entrepreneurs' investment demand, and therefore the demand for the nontradable input. As a result, the price of that input—p^t—increases, which in turn reduces entrepreneurs' borrowing capacity next period, and therefore their output and wealth. Whenever it dominates, this effect will carry the economy from a boom to a slump.

We now show how the combination of these two effects may result in persistent fluctuations, and how the booms and slumps

[2] Here we use the fact that:

$$(a + p^t) y^t = \mu W_B^t,$$

so that:

$$\frac{dy^t}{dW_B^t} = \frac{\mu}{a + p^t} - \frac{y^t}{a + p^t} \frac{\partial p^t}{\partial W_B^t}.$$

in these fluctuations share many features with those observed in practice.

4.2.3 Existence of limit cycles

Figure 4.1 depicts future wealth as a function of current wealth as implied by the dynamic equation (4.3) in the Leontief case. As one can see, the curve consists of three pieces, corresponding respectively to low, intermediate, and high levels of current wealth. Let us look at those three regions in more details.

Suppose first that current wealth W_B^t is sufficiently small that the credit constraint is binding $\left(L = (\mu - 1)W_B^t\right)$ and entrepreneurs do not have enough wealth to use the whole endowment of nontradable input under the Leontief technology $((\mu W_B^t/a) < Z)$. In this case, there is an excess supply of the nontradable input. This immediately yields: $p^t = 0$. Output at date t is then given by:

$$y^t = \frac{K^t}{a} = \frac{\mu W_B^t}{a},$$

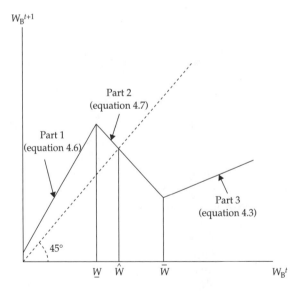

FIG. 4.1 Phase diagram with Leontief technology.
Source: Aghion *et al.* (2004a), figure 1.

so that

$$W_B^{t+1} = (1 - \alpha) \left[e + \frac{\mu W_B^t}{a} - r(\mu - 1) W_B^t \right]. \qquad (4.6)$$

This equation corresponds to the first piece in Figure 4.1. Here no price effect is at work. There is only a wealth effect, and this is why an increase in current wealth leads unambiguously to an increase in future wealth.

Now, suppose that current wealth W_B^t remains sufficiently small that the credit constraint is still binding ($L = (\mu - 1)W_B^t$), but that entrepreneurs now have enough wealth, and therefore enough investment capacity, to exhaust the whole supply of nontradable input under the Leontief technology (i.e. ($K^t/a) \geq Z$). Thus, there is excess demand for the immobile factor. In that case, the equilibrium price p^t of the nontradable input becomes positive, and output is determined in equilibrium by the aggregate supply of that input: $y^t = Z$. From (4.4) and the definition of I, the equilibrium price of the country-specific input is given by:

$$p^t = \frac{\mu W_B^t - aZ}{Z},$$

so that future wealth is now determined by the dynamic equation:

$$W_B^{t+1} = (1 - \alpha) \left[e + Z - r(\mu - 1) W_B^t \right]. \qquad (4.7)$$

This equation corresponds to the second piece in Figure 4.1. There, only the price effect is at work (since output is fixed at $y^t = Z$), which explains why this branch is downward sloping.

Finally, when current wealth W_B^t is sufficiently large enough that entrepreneurs are no longer credit constrained (i.e. $L < (\mu - 1)W_B^t$), then as in the previous case the equilibrium price of the nontradable input p^t is positive and output remains fixed at $y^t = Z$, but the price p^t is no longer affected by the level of investment. When W_B^t is that large, entrepreneurs will borrow until profits equal the international interest rate. In other words, they are indifferent between lending on the international market or investing in their own project, which in turn yields the dynamic equation (4.3). This equation corresponds to the third, again upward sloping, piece in Figure 4.1.

As drawn in Figure 4.1, the 45° line intersects the $W_B^{t+1}(W_B^t)$ curve at the point $\widehat{W}$ which lies in the second segment. This intersection can also be in either of the other two segments. It will be in the first segment when $(1 - \alpha)e/(1 - (1 - \alpha)\{(\mu/a) - r(\mu - 1)\})$, the fixed point of equation (4.6), is less than $\underline{W} = aZ/\mu$. Since $(1 - \alpha)e/(1 - (1 - \alpha)\{(\mu/a) - r(\mu - 1)\})$ is increasing in μ while $\underline{W}$ is decreasing, it is clear that this can only happen when μ is very small. On the other hand, the intersection will be in the third segment when the fixed point of equation (4.3), $(1-\alpha)e/(1-(1-\alpha)r) > \overline{W} = Z/\mu r$. This will only happen when μ is sufficiently large. For intermediate values of μ, corresponding to an intermediate level of financial development, the case is depicted in Figure 4.1. This is the one case where the economy does not converge monotonically to its steady state.

In this case there are two possibilities—*short-run fluctuations*, represented by oscillations that eventually converge to the steady state, $\widehat{W}$, and *long-run volatility*, represented by a system which does not converge to a steady state but instead continues to oscillate forever. A necessary condition for the existence of such a limit cycle is that the steady state at $\widehat{W}$ be unstable, true only when the slope of the $W_B^{t+1}(W_B^t)$ schedule at $\widehat{W}$ is less than -1, corresponding to when $\widehat{W}$ lies in the second segment of that schedule. Thus, for *long-run volatility* to occur, we must have $\underline{W} < \widehat{W} < \overline{W}$ and $-(1 - \alpha)(\mu - 1)r < -1$. If these conditions hold, one can easily derive additional sufficient conditions under which long-run volatility actually occurs. [3]

---

[3] For example, a two-cycle $(W_1 \cdot W_2)$ will satisfy:

$$W_1 = \frac{(1 - \alpha)(e + Z)}{1 + r(\mu - 1)(1 - \alpha)^2(e + (\mu/a) - r(\mu - 1))},$$

$$W_2 = \frac{(1 - \alpha)^2(e + (\mu/a) - r(\mu - 1))(e + Z)}{1 + r(\mu - 1)(1 - \alpha)^2(e + (\mu/a) - r(\mu - 1))},$$

with $W_1 < \underline{W} < W_2 < \overline{W}$. This two-cycle will be stable whenever $(1 - \alpha)^2 r(\mu - 1)((\mu/a) - r(\mu - 1)) < 1$. Conditions for the existence of longer (and more plausible) cycles can be derived using standard techniques. The dynamic simulations will show that the fluctuations can be complex since wealth can fluctuate between the constrained (the first two segments in Figure 4.1) and the unconstrained (the third segment) regions.

Intuitively, the basic mechanism underlying this cyclicality can be described as follows: during a boom the demand for the domestic country-specific factor goes up as (high-yield) investments increase, thus raising its price. This higher price will eventually squeeze investors' borrowing capacity and therefore the demand for country-specific factors. At this point, the economy experiences a slump and two things occur: the relative price of the domestic factor collapses, while a fraction of the factor available remains unused since there is not enough investment. The collapse in the factor price thus corresponds to a contraction of real output. Of course, the low factor price will eventually lead to higher profits and therefore to more investment. A new boom then begins.[4]

The reason why the level of financial development matters is also quite intuitive: economies at a low level of financial development have low levels of investment and do not generate enough demand to push up the price of the country-specific factor while economies at a very high level of development have sufficient demand for that factor to keep its price always positive. It is then at intermediate levels of financial development that shocks to cash flow will have an effect intense enough to be a source of instability.

This last argument also helps us understand why opening the economy to foreign capital may destabilize: essentially, the response of an economy with a closed capital market to a cash flow shock is limited since only so much capital is available to entrepreneurs. Additional funding sources in an open economy

---

[4] One may wonder to which extent the basic mechanism leading to volatility here relies on the assumption of discrete time. It is well known that volatility occurs more easily under discrete time. However, it is not difficult to show that a similar mechanism can occur under continuous time. First, this can happen with a system of two differential equations. For example, if domestic lenders are also workers paid by the entrepreneurs and use the local input for their consumption, then a second dynamic equation describing the evolution of domestic lenders' wealth must be added to the dynamic equation describing the evolution of domestic entrepreneurs' wealth. If domestic lenders' demand for the local input is not too price elastic, we still get the same type of volatility as in the basic model with a single difference equation. Second, Bruchez (2001) shows that if the lags between the wealth realization in period t and the wealth investment in period $t + 1$ differ across firms, equation (4.2) becomes an ordinary differential equation that can also exhibit periodic solutions. This result obtains when the discrete lags are randomly gamma distributed, as shown in Invernizzi and Medio (1991).

potentially increase the response to a shock and therefore the scope for volatility.

4.3 Confronting the theory with some facts

Although the above framework is extremely simple, it generates a number of predictions for empirical analysis on emerging markets. In particular, our model predicts that:

1. *The investment to GDP and private credit to GDP ratios should increase during a "lending boom."* To see this in the context of the above model, just note that:

$$\frac{\mu W_B^t}{y^t} = \frac{I^t}{y^t} = a + p^t,$$

   which indeed increases during a lending boom as a result of the price effect;

2. *Lending booms are times of net capital inflows;* this in turn follows from the fact that the capital account (or net capital flow) at any date t, is equal to:

$$CA_t = W_B^t + W_L^t - \mu W_B^t,$$

   so that

$$\frac{dCA_t}{dW_B^t} = \frac{dW_L^t}{dW_B^t} - (\mu - 1),$$

   which is indeed negative if, as one would reasonably expect in a small open economy, domestic savings are only weakly correlated with borrowers' wealth;

3. *The real exchange rate should increase during a lending boom;* this immediately follows from the real exchange rate being simply equal to p^t in our model;

4. *The probability of default should increase during a lending boom;* this conclusion obtains in a straightforward extension of our model with output uncertainty and defaults, which we develop in Aghion *et al.* (2004a).

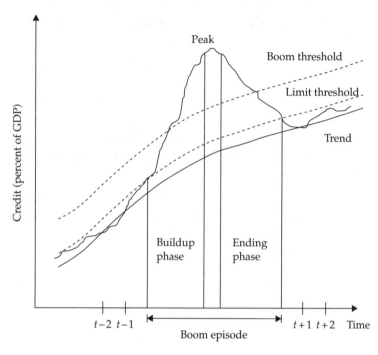

Fig. 4.2 Definition of a lending boom episode.
Source: GVL (2001), figure 1.

Recent work by Gourinchas–Valdés–Landerretche (2001), henceforth GVL, provides strong empirical support for all of these predictions. First, they define a lending boom as "a deviation of the ratio between nominal private credit and nominal GDP from a rolling retrospective country-specific stochastic trend." This definition encompasses the booms in our model. As shown in Figure 4.2, each lending boom comprises a buildup phase during which the credit to GDP ratio increases beyond its long-run trend, a peak phase where the credit stops growing faster than GDP, and finally an ending phase during which the credit to GDP ratio decreases below its long-run trend.

Second, they consider a cross-country sample comprising 91 countries over the period 1960–96. They measure private credit by the amount of claims of nonbanking institutions from banking institutions, and they estimate the trend of the corresponding credit to GDP ratio by using a rolling Hodrick–Prescott filter for each country.

The behavior of macroeconomic indicators such as aggregate output, investment to GDP, private credit, the current account, and the real exchange rate is shown to be fully consistent with the above predictions. In particular: (i) Figure 4.3 shows that the ratio of private credit to GDP increases sharply during the buildup phase of a lending boom; (ii) Figure 4.4 shows a similar pattern for the investment to GDP ratio, which also increases sharply during the buildup phase of a lending boom and then decreases during the ending phase; (iii) Figure 4.5 shows that the current account decreases and becomes negative during the buildup phase

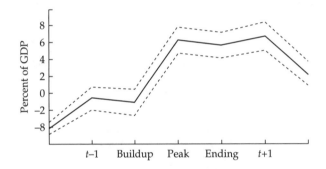

Fɪɢ. 4.3 Private credit/GDP.
Source: GVL (2001), figure 6.1.

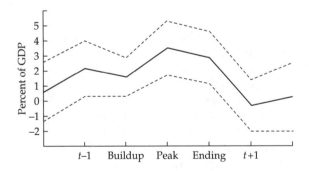

Fɪɢ. 4.4 Investment/GDP.
Source: GVL (2001), figure 6.4.

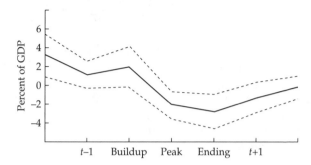

FIG. 4.5 Current account/GDP.
Source: GVL (2001), figure 6.11.

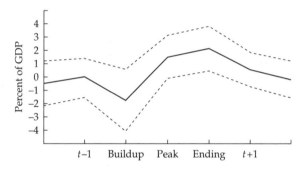

FIG. 4.6 Private capital flows/GDP.
Source: GVL (2001), figure 6.13.

and then increases again during the ending phase; (iv) Figure 4.6 shows that the inflow of private capital is (increasingly) posit-ive during the buildup phase, but reverses to negative later on; (v) Figure 4.7 shows that the real exchange rate increases dur-ing the buildup phase and decreases during the ending phase; (vi) Figure 4.8 shows that the interest spread—which is positively correlated with the likelihood of defaults—increases during the buildup phase and decreases during the ending phase, although GVL point out that this pattern is not significant.

By comparing with "tranquil periods," GVL show that during lending booms the output gap is higher, the investment/GDP ratio increases, the proportion of short-term debt increases, the current account worsens, and the real exchange rate appreciates, especially

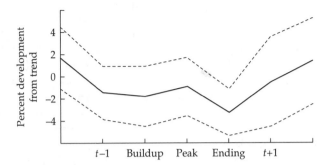

FIG. 4.7 Real exchange rate.
Source: GVL (2001), figure 6.12.

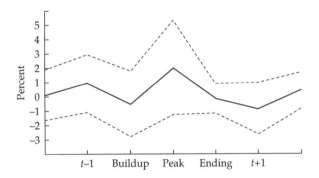

FIG. 4.8 Interest rate spread.
Source: GVL (2001), figure 6.7.

at the end of the boom period. When lending declines, all these movements are reversed. In particular, the fact that investment follows a credit expansion and is sharply procyclical is fully consistent with our approach.

4.4 Financial liberalization and instability

The previous analysis shows that a fully open economy with imperfect credit markets can exhibit volatility or a cycle. We show in this section that the same economy can be stable if it is closed to capital flows or if only foreign direct investment (FDI) is allowed. Thus, a full liberalization to capital movements may destabilize an economy: while it stabilizes the real interest rate, it also amplifies the fluctuations in the price of the country-specific factor. This in turn, increases the volatility in firms' cash flows and therefore aggregate output. We first consider the case of an economy that opens up to foreign lending. Then, we examine the case of FDI, where foreign investors are equity holders and are fully informed about domestic firms. Even though the results are valid with general production functions, we present the Leontief case for pedagogical reasons.

4.4.1 Liberalizing foreign borrowings

We consider an economy with low domestic savings, with the Leontief technology specified in Section 4.2, and we first assume that this economy is *not* open to foreign borrowing and lending.[5] In that case, at each date, the current wealth of domestic lenders W_L matters since domestic investment is constrained by domestic savings $W_B + W_L$. Now suppose that the initial levels of wealth held by entrepreneurs and domestic lenders, W_B and W_L respectively, are sufficiently small so that initially $p^0 = 0$. This corresponds to a situation where domestic entrepreneurs cannot exhaust the supply of country-specific inputs. Let us also assume that at date 0 domestic savings $W_B^0 + W_L^0$ are less than the investment capacity μW_B^0.[6] If $\mu > 1$ there will then be excess investment capacity in subsequent periods as long as p^t remains equal to 0. To see this, note that the domestic interest rate r^t, determined in a closed economy by the comparison between W_L^t and $(\mu - 1)W_B^t$, is such that entrepreneurs are indifferent between borrowing and lending, that is: $r^t = 1/a$ in the Leontief case. Therefore, if $p^t = 0$ and $W_L^t < (\mu - 1)W_B^t$,

---

[5] This closed economy is described in detail in Appendix A of Aghion *et al.* (2004a).

[6] If $\mu W_B < W_L$, opening up the economy to foreign lending would make no difference: since the investment capacity of domestic entrepreneurs cannot even absorb domestic savings, there is no need for foreign lending in this case.

we have:

$$W_B^{t+1} = (1 - \alpha) \left[e + \frac{1}{a} W_B^t \right]$$

$$\text{and } W_L^{t+1} = (1 - \alpha) \left[e + \frac{1}{a} W_L^t \right],$$

so that $W_L^t < (\mu - 1) W_B^t$ implies that: $W_L^{t+1} < (\mu - 1) W_B^{t+1}$ and therefore $r^{t+1} = 1/a$. In Aghion *et al.* (2004a) we provide sufficient conditions under which $p^t = 0$ and $r^t = 1/a$ for all t. Under these conditions, entrepreneurs' wealth will grow at the (low) rate $(1 - \alpha)/a$, since it is constrained by the (low) level of domestic savings, and the W_B^{t+1} (W_B^t) schedule will intersect the 45° line on its first branch along which $p^t = 0$. This, in turn, implies that there will be no persistent fluctuations in this closed economy.

What happens if this economy is fully opened up to foreign borrowing and lending? The interest rate will be fixed at the international level r. By itself, this could only help stabilize any closed economy that otherwise might (temporarily) fluctuate in reaction to interest rate movements. However, the opening up of the economy to foreign lending also brings net capital inflows as investors satisfy their excess funds demand in international capital markets. The corresponding rise in borrowing in turn increases the scope for bidding up the price of the country-specific factor, thereby inducing permanent fluctuations in p, W_B and aggregate output.

Figure 4.9 presents an illustration of the impact of liberalization. The wealth schedule shifts up after a capital account liberalization. $\widehat{W}_B$ refers to the stable steady-state level of borrowers' wealth before the economy opens up to foreign borrowing and lending. After the liberalization W_B progressively increases as capital inflows allow investors to increase their borrowing, investments, and profits. During the first two periods following the liberalization, the demand for the country-specific factor remains sufficiently low so that $p = 0$. In period 3 (at W_B^3) p increases but we still have growth. However, in period 4 (at W_B^4) the price effect of the liberalization becomes sufficiently strong as to squeeze investors' net worth, thereby bringing on a recession. At that point, aggregate lending drops, capital flows out and the real exchange depreciates (p drops). The resulting gain in competitiveness allows firms to rebuild their net worth so that growth can

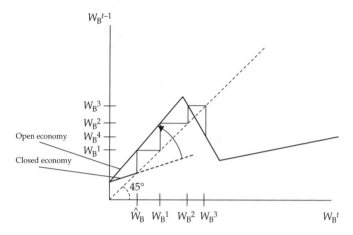

Fɪɢ. 4.9 Liberalizing foreign lending.
Source: Aghion *et al.* (2004a), figure 4.

eventually resume. The economy ends up experiencing permanent fluctuations of the kind described in the previous section.

We should stress that the dynamics in Figure 4.9 occurs only for *intermediate* levels of financial development. As we argued in Section 4.2, with a large μ there is no volatility in an open economy, as it is the third segment of the curve that cuts the 45° line. When $\mu = 1$, financial opening will not help investment and no capital inflow will occur, so there will be no upward pressure on the price of the country-specific input.[7] The above example therefore suggests that it might be desirable for a country to increase its μ, that is, to develop its domestic financial sector *before* fully opening up to foreign lending.

4.4.2 *Foreign direct investment*

Whilst a full liberalization to foreign lending can have destabilizing effects on economies with intermediate levels of financial development, those economies are unlikely to become volatile as a result of opening up to foreign *direct* investment alone. We distinguish FDI from other financial flows by assuming that it is

[7] This may be the case in some of the poorer African and Asian countries.

part of firms' equity.[8] Furthermore, we first concentrate on the benchmark case where the supply of FDI is infinitely elastic at some fixed price greater than the world interest rate, say equal to $r + \delta$.[9]

Starting from a situation in which domestic cash flows are small so that domestic investment cannot fully absorb the supply of country-specific factors, foreign direct investors are likely to enter in order to profit from the low price of the country-specific factors. This price will eventually increase and may even fluctuate as a result of FDI. But these price fluctuations will only affect the distribution of profits between domestic and foreign investors, not aggregate output. For example, in the Leontief case with FDI, aggregate output will stabilize at a level equal to the supply of factor resources Z, whereas the same economy may end up being destabilized if fully open to foreign *portfolio* investment (i.e. to foreign lending).

Consider a closed Leontief economy open to FDI only. Assume also that W_L is large enough so that firms can still borrow their desired amount domestically (otherwise investment is still constrained by savings and the scope for fluctuations is much smaller). Then FDI will flow into the economy as long as the rate of return on that investment remains greater than or equal to $r + \delta$. Thus, if F denotes the net inflow of direct investment, in equilibrium we obtain the free-entry condition:

$$F > 0 \Rightarrow R = r + \delta,$$

where $R = (y - \widetilde{r}L)/(W_B + F)$ is the net rate of return on FDI and $\widetilde{r}$ is the domestic interest rate. If domestic savings are less than the investment capacity of domestic entrepreneurs (i.e. $W_L < (\mu - 1)W_B$), we would have $\widetilde{r} = 1/a$. However, as domestic savings exceed the investment capacity of domestic entrepreneurs, $\widetilde{r} = \underline{\sigma}$, where $\underline{\sigma}$ is the return of an alternative, inefficient, storing technology (as in the previous chapter). In a closed economy, lenders will invest their excess savings in this technology.

---

[8] Typically, measured FDI implies participations of more than 10% in a firm's capital so this appears to be a reasonable assumption. Razin *et al.* (1998) make a similar distinction about FDI.

[9] This, in turn, implies that in our model FDI is a substitute to domestic investment. The effects of FDI on macroeconomic volatility when domestic and foreign investments are complementary, are discussed at the end of this section.

Assume that $R > r + \delta$ as long as $p = 0$ (this implies $r + \delta <$ $(1/a)\mu - (\mu - 1)\underline{\sigma}$), so that there will be a positive flow of FDI as long as $p = 0$. Using the fact that $L = (\mu-1)(W_B+F)$ and that $y = Z$ when $p > 0$, we can rewrite the above free-entry condition as:

$$(r + \delta)(W_B + F) = Z - (\mu - 1)\underline{\sigma}(W_B + F).$$

This, together with the price equation (4.7), implies that:

$$p = \frac{\mu}{r + \delta + \underline{\sigma}(\mu - 1)} - a,$$

which in turn defines gives a stable value for p. Thus, even though FDI leads to a price increase it does not generate price and output volatility.

Consider now an economy which has already been opened up to foreign borrowing and lending at rate r, that is to foreign portfolio flows only, and which, as a result has become volatile as in the example depicted in Figure 4.9. What will happen if this economy is now also opening up to FDI? By the same reasoning as before, opening up to FDI will stabilize the price of the country-specific factor at level p^* such that:

$$(r + \delta)(W_B + F) = Z - r(\mu - 1)(W_B + F).$$

This again will eliminate investment and output volatility in this economy (assuming that initially the country is attracting FDI). In other words, if there are no limitations on FDI inflows and out-flows (and FDI involves complete information on domestic firms), the price of the country-specific factor and therefore aggregate domestic GDP or GNP will remain constant in equilibrium.

The reason why FDI acts as a stabilizing force is again that, unlike foreign lending, it does not depend on the creditworthiness of the domestic firms, and furthermore it is precisely during slumps that foreign direct investors may prefer to come in so as to benefit from the low price of the country-specific factor.

What happens if FDI is *complementary* to domestic direct invest-ment, that is, to W_B? Such complementarity may be due to legal restrictions whereby the total amount of FDI cannot be greater than a fixed fraction x of domestic investors' wealth W_B, or it may stem from the need for local investors to enforce dividend payments or to help exert control. Aghion *et al.* show that FDI subject to complementarity requirements of the form $F \leq xW_B$, may sometimes *de*-stabilize an emerging market economy. Indeed, in contrast to the unrestricted FDI case analyzed above, such direct investments ultimately will fall during slumps, that is, when investors' wealth W_B^{t+1} is experiencing a downturn. Downturns will also typically be deeper than in the absence of FDI since, by amplifying the increase in p^t during booms, FDI increases production costs and thus accentuates the credit-crunch induced on firms. Thus, while unrestricted FDI has a stabilizing effect on an open emerging market economy, opening such an economy to restricted FDI may actually have the opposite effect.

4.5 Policy conclusions

The model in this and the previous chapter provide simple and tractable frameworks for analyzing financially based crises in economies which are at an intermediate level of financial development. The story we tell is based on some very basic features of these economies, in contrast with other more institutionally based theories which invoke moral hazard among lenders, herd behavior among investors, etc. This is not to say that our model is inconsistent with this class of theories but our model does suggest a rather specific policy response: Slumps in our model are a part of the normal process in economies like these, which are at an intermediate level of financial development and are in the process of liberalizing their financial sectors. We should therefore not overreact to the occurrence of financial crises, especially in the case of emerging market economies. In particular, hasty and radical overhauling of their economic system may do more harm than good.[10]

---

[10] Indeed, if our model is right, the slump sets in motion forces which, even with little interference, should eventually bring growth back to these economies. The risk is that by trying to overhaul the system in a panic, one may actually undermine those forces of recovery instead of stimulating them. This is not to deny that there is a lot that needs changing in these economies, especially on the institutional side with the establishment and enforcement of disciplinary rules in credit and banking activities. For example, in the context of our model, banks may typically

Second, policies allowing firms to rebuild their creditworthiness quickly will at the same time contribute to a prompt recovery of the overall economy. In this context it is worth considering the role for monetary policy and, more generally, for policies affecting the credit market. While our model in its present form cannot be *directly* used for analyzing monetary policy since money is neutral in this model (and in any case the interest rate is fixed by the world interest rate), it can be extended to allow for both monetary nonneutrality and a less elastic supply of foreign loans. This is what we do in the next chapter (based on Aghion *et al.* 2000, 2001).

This emphasis on creditworthiness as the key element in the recovery from a slump, also suggests that a policy of allowing insolvent banks to fail may in fact prolong the slump if it restricts firms' ability to borrow (because of the comparative advantage of banks in monitoring firms' activities[11]). If banks must be shut down, there should be an effort to preserve their monitoring expertise on the relevant industries. Moreover, to the extent that the government has to spend resources on restructuring and cleaning-up after a spate of bankruptcies, it should avoid raising taxes during a slump, since doing so would further limit the borrowing capacity of domestic entrepreneurs and therefore delay the subsequent recovery.

Third, our model also delivers *ex ante* policy implications for emerging market economies not currently under a financial crisis. In particular: (i) an unrestricted financial liberalization may actually *destabilize* the economy and engender a slump that would otherwise not have happened. If a major slump is likely to be costly even in the long run (because, for example, it sets in process destabilizing political forces), fully liberalizing foreign capital flows and fully opening the economy to foreign lending may not be a good idea at least until the domestic financial sector is sufficiently well developed (i.e. until the credit-multiplier μ becomes sufficiently large); (ii) FDI does *not* destabilize. Indeed, as we have argued above, FDI is most likely to come in during slumps when

---

engage in preemptive lending to speculators in domestic inputs and/or to producers during booms. This in turn will further increase output volatility whenever inadequate monitoring and expertise acquisition by banks increases aggregate risk and therefore the interest rate imposed upon domestic producers.

[11] See Diamond (1984).

the relative price of the country-specific factor is low; furthermore, even if this price ends up fluctuating when the economy is open to FDI, these fluctuations will only affect the distribution of profits between domestic and foreign investors but not aggregate output. Therefore there is no cost a priori to allowing FDI even at low levels of financial development;[12] (iii) what brings about financial crises is precisely the rise in the price of the country specific factors. If one of these factors (say, real estate) is identified to play a key role in sparking a financial crisis, it would be sensible to control its price, either directly or though controlling its speculative demand using suitable fiscal deterrents. This, and other important aspects in the design of stabilization policies for emerging market economies, await future elaborations of the framework developed in this chapter.

[12] This strategy of allowing only FDI at early stages of financial development is in fact what most developed countries have done, in particular in Europe where restrictions on cross-country capital movements have only been fully removed in the late 1980s, whereas FDI to—and between—European countries had been allowed since the late 1950s.

5

The Third Generation Approach to Currency Crises

THE previous chapter described a world where a financial accelerator first generates a lending driven boom and then its inevitable collapse. But that collapse contains within itself the seeds of a new boom; and so the economy continues, bouncing from boom to crisis and back.

The evidence, described in the previous chapter, from GVL (2001), is primarily about what happens when a lending boom collapses. As we saw it fits well with what happens in our model. It does not however say very much about the recovery; in particular they have nothing to say about whether the economy actually bounces back all the way. The concern that this may not always be the case comes from the finding, reported in GVL (2001) that lending booms tend to increase the probability of a currency crisis,[1] combined with the evidence that after currency crises countries do not go back to the pre-crisis trend. Figure 5.1, taken from Griffith-Jones (2004) illustrates this point for the case of Indonesia. By extrapolating the preexisting trend in GDP and comparing with post-crisis outcomes, Griffith-Jones estimates that between 1995 and 2002 (admittedly a period when crises where both very damaging and very frequent), the annual cost of crises for Argentina, Brazil, Indonesia, Korea, Malaysia, Mexico, Thailand, and Turkey combined reached the very large estimated amount of US$ 150 billion (in 2002 US$). Eichengreen (2004) looks at a longer period and estimates the cost of currency crises at 0.7% of developing country emerging market GDP per year, equivalent to an annual amount of US$ 107 billion, or to put it differently, over the last quarter century, currency and banking crises have reduced incomes of developing countries by around 25%.

---

[1] GVL define a currency crisis as a nominal devaluation that exceeds 25% on a year-to-year basis.

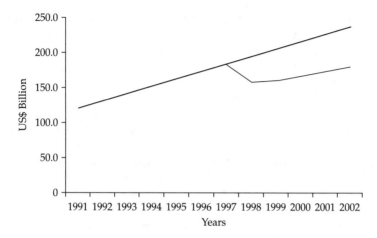

FIG. 5.1 Indonesia: potential and actual GDP.

Note: Projected output for the years 1997–2002 based on output trend over the 1991–6 period. Values are in US$ 1989 billion. Data source: World Bank data base.

Source: Griffith-Jones (2004), figure 1.

In this chapter we present a highly stylized model, based, as in previous chapters, on limited access to credit,[2] that can explain why an economy that is carrying a large amount of foreign currency debt might be vulnerable to currency crises, which leave it with a depreciated currency and GDP that remains lower than the pre-crisis trend for some time into the future. We are about to argue that, in a monetary economy with standard price rigidities, credit constraints together with pecuniary externalities working through the nominal exchange rate are sufficient to generate currency crises.

---

[2] We refer our advanced readers to Aghion *et al.* (2004b) for a fully microfounded third generation approach to currency crises, based on the same basic idea. In that model: (i) consumption and savings decisions are based on intertemporal utility maximization; (ii) foreign currency borrowing is endogeneized; (iii) banks' demand for reserves is also endogeneized and linked to their supply of credit to the manufacturing sector; (iv) price shocks are anticipated. The paper then derives sufficient conditions under which a sunspot equilibrium with currency crisis exists.

There is, of course, a long tradition of models aimed at helping us understand currency crises. Thus, a first generation of models[3] took the view that currency crises resulted from large budget deficits. While this explanation could fit the case of Latin American countries in the 1980s, it can hardly account for why currency crises occurred in East and South-east Asia in the late 1990s, since governments in this region were all running budget surpluses. A second generation[4] attributes the occurrence of currency crises to credibility problems faced by governments with the conflicting objectives of maintaining a fixed exchange rate parity and reducing unemployment. While this could explain the collapse of the European Monetary System in the early 1990s, the unemployment rates in the Asian economies of the 1990s were among the lowest in the world, and it is hard to believe that reducing unemployment was a priority for these governments. Our view of the crisis falls into the class of "third generation" theories: These are theories which locate the proximate source of the crisis in the private sector rather than in the government.[5]

The basic mechanism that generates crises is simply summarized as follows: if nominal prices are rigid in the short run, a currency depreciation leads to an increase in the foreign currency debt repayment obligations of firms. In a setting where the firm sector has a large outstanding foreign debt, for example because of a lending boom in the preceding few years, this can have a very substantial impact on profits and the net worth of the firm sector.[6] This in turn limits the firms' ability to borrow and therefore may result in less investment and lower output in the next period. The resulting fall in the demand for money will cause the currency to depreciate in the next period. But arbitrage in the foreign exchange market then implies that the currency must depreciate

---

[3] For example, see Krugman (1999), Furman and Stiglitz (1998), Radelet and Sachs (1998).

[4] See Obstfeld (1994).

[5] See Aghion *et al.* (2000, 2004b), Krugman (1999), Chang and Velasco (1999).

[6] The damaging impact of foreign currency debt is often mentioned in the context of currency crises. See, for example, Cooper (1971), Calvo (1998), and Mishkin (1996, 1999). While the role of foreign currency *public* debt has received some attention in the theoretical literature on crises (e.g. Bohn 1990; Obstfeld 1994; Falcetti and Missale 1999), the impact of private foreign currency debt has hardly been analyzed (see, however, Jeanne 2000a).

in the current period as well. In other words, if people believe that the currency will depreciate, it may indeed depreciate. In other words, when the firm sector is carrying a large amount of foreign currency debt, there are multiple short-run equilibria in the market for foreign exchange. What we call currency crises are shifts between "good" equilibria and "bad" equilibria, triggered by a change in expectations or a real shock to the economy.

This story of currency crises has the significant advantage that it is based on two well-known facts: first, the countries most likely to go into a crisis were those in which firms held a lot of foreign currency denominated debt. For example, Figure 5.2 shows the ratio of claims to liabilities with respect to BIS banks; since these transactions are mostly in foreign currency, this ratio is a measure of aggregate foreign currency exposure. It is striking that all the countries that had a ratio higher than 1.5 have experienced a serious crisis in the 1990s. In the next section, we discuss possible rationales for firms to hold foreign currency debt.

The second fact is that there are substantial and persistent deviations from purchasing power parity following an exchange rate shock: Engel (1993) decribes this evidence in some detail. In a recent important paper Burstein *et al.* (2004) have shown that in the case of large devaluations, this is mainly driven by the

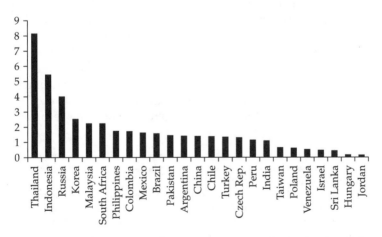

FIG. 5.2 Ratio of liabilities to claims with respect to foreign banks 1997.
Source: Aghion *et al.* (2001), figure 1.

nonadjustment of the prices of nontradables; this filters into the price of tradables in part because of distribution costs and in part because people move to cheaper, less traded, goods.[7]

This means that for our story to go through, the firms producing nontraded goods must be carrying foreign currency debt. The same evidence shows that a very large part of GDP is effectively nontraded which makes this more likely. For example, there is no reason why foreign currency debt is more likely to be held by a firm that produces a tradable, than by the firm that builds or owns warehouses that store the tradable good. While there are many very small firms in the nontraded sector, there are also many very large firms, especially in construction and distribution.

Our credit-based approach to currency crises also has the advantage of being consistent with the observation that countries with less developed financial systems are more likely to experience an output decline during a crisis.[8] Second, it makes it clear why a currency crisis can also happen under a flexible exchange rate or without any significant decline in foreign exchange reserves. Third, crises may occur even in countries that are conventionally well-behaved, in the sense of having low unemployment rates and conservative fiscal and monetray policies.

It still remains that public policy variables such as fiscal deficits, influence whether a currency crisis occurs, as stressed by the existing literature on the subject. However, in contrast to first- and second generation models, in the world described in this chapter a deterioration of fiscal balances will lead to a crisis mainly through its impact on private firms' balance sheets rather than through simple money demand adjustments as in the previous models.[9] Moreover, the presence of public sector debt may exacerbate the problems of private sector debt, especially if a large fraction of public sector debt is in foreign currency. This result is in

---

[7] With smaller devaluations, such as the ones in the United States in recent years, this is less true. Slow adjustment of tradables is a significant part of the nonadjustment (see Engel 1999).

[8] It is indeed striking that several countries that experienced a large depreciation in the ERM crisis in 1992–3 had a relatively good output performance; while others, like Finland, and countries that suffered from the Mexican and Asian crises faced serious recessions.

[9] Surveys of the currency crises literature include Garber and Svensson (1995), Obstfeld and Rogoff (1996), Flood and Marion (1998), and Tirole (2002).

sharp contrast with the previous literature that argues that foreign currency (public) debt should have a stabilizing effect.

Another advantage of our model is that it lends itself very naturally to the analysis of monetary policy. There has been an important debate on the stance of monetary policy in the context of currency crises; one side in this debate emphasizes the importance of past government failures and advocates monetary tightening, in part to signal the government's commitment to restraint.[10] The other side blames shifts in expectations and bad luck (the multiple equilibrium view) and sees no reason why we should punish the already battered firm sector even more by tightening monetary policy.[11] Strikingly, though our model is of the multiple equilibrium kind, as long as the credit multiplier only depends on *real* interest rates and prices adjust relatively quickly, a restrictive monetary policy is the optimal response to the risk of a currency crisis. This is because the shift in exchange rates generated by tightening remains the best way to help the beleagured firm sector. However, we also show that this conclusion may cease to hold when credit supply is affected by the *nominal* interest rate and/or when price adjustment takes longer than it takes to discharge the inherited debt obligations of the firm sector.

The rest of the chapter is organized as follows. Section 5.1 lays out the basic model. Section 5.2 shows that this model naturally gives itself to graphical analysis. Using this graphical apparatus we examine the occurrence of currency crises and demonstrate the possibility of multiple equilibria. Section 5.3 analyzes the policy implications of the model, and Section 5.4 concludes.

5.1 The basic model

A more fully-fledged and microfounded version of the model in this section is developed in Aghion *et al.* (2004b). While we chose

[10] This view has been consistently advocated by the IMF. In particular, Stanley Fischer argued that "those who criticize temporary high interest rates fail to see that further depreciation caused by lower rates would have raised the burden of dollar-denominated debts."

[11] See, for example, Radelet and Sachs (1998) and Furman and Stiglitz (1998).

to present a reduced form version for pedagogical purposes, we highly encourage the reader to then move to the microfounded version which also contains a more elaborate policy discussion.

We consider an infinite-horizon small open economy monetary model where goods prices are determined at the beginning of each period and remain fixed for the entire period.[12] There is a single tradable good and purchasing power parity (PPP) holds *ex ante*, that is, $P_t = E_t^e$ for each t, where P_t is the domestic price set by firms, E_t^e is the expected nominal exchange rate (the price of foreign currency in terms of domestic currency) at the beginning of period t, and the foreign price is constant and equal to 1. Prices are preset for one period.

A key ingredient of our model will be a shock in period 1 that occurs *after* the price in that period has been set. This shock may be real—such as a change in productivity or competitiveness or the risk perceptions of bondholders at home or abroad. Or it may be a pure shift in expectations—as is well-known, in a world of multiple equilibria, such shifts can have real effects.[13] The shock causes a deviation from PPP *ex post* in period 1, that is[14]:

$$P_1 \neq E_1.$$

Since prices cannot move during period 1, the nominal exchange rate has to move to absorb the shock.[15] These deviations will play a crucial role in the analysis.

[12] The assumption that prices are preset for one period is commonly made in monetary models of an open economy, following Obstfeld and Rogoff (1995).

[13] For most of the chapter we assume that the shock is wholly unanticipated and is not taken into account by the domestic market when setting the date-1 price. This assumption is commonly made by the existing models of open monetary macroeconomics (see again Obstfeld and Rogoff, 1995). However, our results hold when the distribution of expectational shocks is taken into account *ex ante*, as shown in Aghion *et al.* (2004b).

[14] In Aghion *et al.* (2004b) we concentrate on the existence of rational expectation sunspot equilibria in which P_1 is equal to the expected exchange rate in period 1, that is:

$$P_1 = E(E_1).$$

[15] Producers set prices in domestic currency by taking the foreign price (adjusted by the expected exchange rate) as given. In contrast to some recent models in the so-called "New Open Economy Macroeconomics," we implicitly assume perfect competition on the product market.

The analysis in this chapter relies in a fundamental way upon two basic assumptions about credit markets. First, we assume that credit markets are imperfect. As in the previous chapters, entrepreneurs cannot borrow more than a fixed multiple mw_t of their current real wealth w_t. Entrepreneurs' wealth thus remains the fundamental state variable that determines investment and output. Second, we assume that firms hold foreign currency debt, whose servicing cost for domestic borrowers thus varies with the nominal exchange rate. This in turn introduces the pecuniary externality part of the story.

While this latter assumption accords well with what we observe in many emerging market economies, it requires a justification. In Schneider and Tornell (2000) foreign currency borrowing follows from the assumption that domestic banks are bailed out by the government in case of default, so that firms will want to increase their risk of exposure by borrowing in foreign currency. Jeanne (2000a,b) develops models in which foreign currency borrowing serves as a signaling or as a commitment device. In Chamon and Hausmann (2002) and Aghion *et al.* (2001) foreign currency borrowing follows directly from extrinsic exchange rate uncertainty together with the assumption that the currency composition of a borrower's portfolio is not contractible: in that case, if a first lender decided to lend in domestic currency, the borrower could use the amount of the loan as a collateral to borrow from a second borrower in foreign currency; then, a large currency depreciation together with limited liability would allow the borrower to (partly) default on the first lender. Anticipating this, the first lender would charge an interest rate that makes it a weakly dominated option for the borrower to borrow upfront in foreign currency.

In all other respects the model is quite standard: output is produced using capital, and the production function $y_t = f(k_t)$ has the standard concave shape. There is full capital mobility, and uncovered interest parity holds. The exchange rate can be either floating or fixed, even though the fixed exchange rate case is only explicitly analyzed in Section 5.3. Consumers need money for their transactions, and there is a central bank that can alter interest rates or the exchange rate by affecting money supply.

The timing of events can be summarized as follows. In the first period, the price P_1 is preset and firms invest. Then, an unanticipated shock occurs followed by a monetary adjustment which determines both the nominal interest rate i_1 to be paid at the end of the *second* period (interest rates are always set one period ahead) and the nominal exchange rate E_1 (when the latter is not maintained fixed). Subsequently, period 1's output and profits are generated and firms' debts are repaid. Finally, a fraction $(1 - \alpha)$ of net retained earnings after debt repayment, namely w_2, is saved for investment in period 2.[16] Periods after period 1 are identical in all respects except in that after period 2, no further shock occurs and the economy converges to its steady state.

The remaining part of this section, first, describes the monetary side of the economy and, second, analyzes the entrepreneurs' borrowing and production decisions.

5.1.1 The monetary sector

The interaction between consumers, foreign investors, and the central bank gives us both a money market equilibrium condition (i.e. an LM curve) and an interest parity (IP) condition (i.e. an IP curve). Since both types of conditions are standard in open economy macroeconomics, we shall not expand on their microfoundations.[17] Arbitrage by investors between domestic and foreign currency bonds in a world with perfect capital mobility yields the following IP condition:

$$1 + i_t = (1 + i^*)\frac{E_{t+1}^e}{E_t} \tag{5.1}$$

where i^* is the foreign interest rate which we assume to be constant over time.

In addition, consumers have a standard real money demand function $m_t^d = m^d(y_t, i_t)$. The function m^d has the usual properties of being increasing in y_t and decreasing in i_t;[18] furthermore,

---

[16] In Aghion *et al.* (2004b), we instead derive consumption and savings from intertemporal utility maximization.

[17] For example, see Krugman and Obstfeld (2000) and Blanchard (1996) for pedagogical presentations of the LM and IP relationships. For a more detailed and microfounded modeling of the monetary sector, once again we refer our reader to Aghion *et al.* (2004b).

[18] This follows from consumers' arbitrage between holding money for transaction purposes and holding (domestic) bonds that yield interest rate i_t.

we assume: $m^d(0, i_t) > 0$.[19] Thus, at any date t, money market equilibrium can be expressed by the $(LM)_t$ equation:

$$M_t^S = P_t \cdot m^d(y_t, i_t) \tag{5.2}$$

where M_t^S is the nominal money supply at date t. Let z_t denote the rate of nominal money supply growth between periods $t - 1$ and t, so that: $M_t^S = (1 + z_t)M_{t-1}^S$. Computing the growth rate of equation (5.2), we can determine the evolution of the inflation rate π_t:

$$1 + \pi_t = (1 + z_t)\frac{m_{t-1}^d}{m_t^d} \tag{5.3}$$

Equation (5.3) holds for all periods without shocks, in our analysis for $t \geq 2$. In period 1, since price P_1 is preset, it is the interest rate i_1 that adjusts to equilibrate the money market. Thus, equation (5.2) yields:

$$i_1 = \phi(M_1^S, y_1) \tag{5.4}$$

where ϕ is the inverse of the m^d function with respect to i. The relationship between i_1 and M_1^S is unambiguously negative due to the standard liquidity effect. Thus, either of the two variables can be used to discuss the effects of monetary policy in period 1.

5.1.2 Output and entrepreneurs' debt

Since capital is the only production input and fully depreciates within one period, entrepreneurs' capital stock at the beginning of each period t is: $k_t = w_t + d_t$, where d_t stands for the demand for debt. Thus, current output becomes a function of current entrepreneurs' wealth whenever the credit constraint is binding, namely:

$$y_t = f(\mu w_t).$$

When the constraint is not binding ($d_t < mw_t$), the levels of borrowing and output are simply given by the standard first-order condition: $f'(k_t) = 1 + i^*$.

---

[19] This last assumption is needed in our context since output only depends on past profits and therefore can be equal to 0. It can be dropped in a more general context, for example, when we introduce a competitiveness effect.

When crises are anticipated, the key issue is whether the endogeneity of currency exposure would eliminate the possibility of a crisis. Note that when the borrower chooses the currency composition of his own debt, he takes as given the composition of debt in the rest of the economy—he will not deviate from his privately optimal choice of currency composition to prevent a crisis. He may have private reasons for preferring domestic currency debt if there is some chance of a crisis, especially if default is costly for him. However, given that he cannot prevent the crisis by making this choice, moving to domestic debt simply shifts the risk on to the lender, who will accept it only if the price the borrower pays for the insurance (in terms of foregone benefits from holding foreign currency debt as well as the cost of compensating the lender for the extra risk he bears) is worthwhile; this would only be the case if a crisis were sufficiently likely. It follows that if all the other borrowers were to choose levels of d_t^c that are such that no crisis is possible, an individual borrower would simply choose the level of domestic currency debt, d_t^c, that is optimal for him without the possibility of a crisis. If this preferred level of foreign currency debt happens to be higher than the minimum needed to make a crisis possible, the only equilibrium value of d_t^c is one where there will sometime be a crisis. Note that this reasoning is valid independently of the reason for which borrowers hold foreign currency debt.

Given the currency composition of domestic entrepreneurs' debt, we can now express their aggregate nominal profits net of debt repayments at the end of any period t, namely:

$$\Pi_t = P_t y_t - (1 + i_{t-1})P_{t-1}d_t^c - (1 + i^*)\frac{E_t}{E_{t-1}}P_{t-1}(d_t - d_t^c).$$

Whenever profits are positive, entrepreneurs retain a proportion $(1 - \alpha)$ of profits and use them to finance their future investment (a proportion α of profits is distributed and/or consumed). Total net wealth available for the next production period $t + 1$ is thus equal either to 0, when net profits at date t are negative, or to:

$$w_{t+1} = (1 - \alpha)\frac{\Pi_t}{P_t}.$$

It follows that second period output y_2, which is a function of the wealth w_2 available at the beginning of period 2, is given by:

$$y_2 = f\left(\mu(1-\alpha)\left\{y_1 - (1+r_0)d_1^c - (1+i^*)\frac{E_1}{P_1}(d_1 - d_1^c)\right\}\right) \quad (5.5)$$

where r_0 is the real interest rate defined as $1 + r_t = (1 + i_t)P_t/P_{t+1}$ and $0 < y_2 < \tilde{y}$. Equation (5.5) clearly shows that output would react negatively to an increase in the debt burden induced by a currency depreciation, that is by an increase in E_1. Note that changes in the nominal interest rate i_1 do not affect the debt burden in period 1 and output in period 2. The reason is simply that i_1 is the interest rate applying to the second period.

However, i_1 will affect the cost of domestic currency debt and therefore the debt burden in period 2 positively, and therefore the output in period 3 negatively. More formally, we have:

$$y_3 = f\left(\mu(1-\alpha)\left\{y_2 - (1+i_1)\frac{P_1}{P_2}d_2^c - (1+i^*)\frac{E_2}{E_1}\frac{P_1}{P_2}(d_2 - d_2^c)\right\}\right). \quad (5.6)$$

In any period $t \geq 3$, the PPP condition continues to hold but in addition the discrepancy between E_1 and P_1 no longer affects the total debt burden of entrepreneurs, that is, domestic and foreign currency debt become fully equivalent. Hence, for $t \geq 3$ output y_{t+1} is simply given by:

$$y_{t+1} = f\left[(1+\mu)(1-\alpha)\left\{y_t - (1+i^*)d_t\right\}\right]. \quad (5.7)$$

The model is now fully laid out. Equilibrium in this model is defined as a sequence of prices (P_t), exchange rates (E_t), and output levels (y_t), which for a given monetary policy in period 1 satisfy the above equations (5.1)–(5.3), (5.5), and (5.7) for all t. The dynamics of aggregate output y_t for $t > 2$, are easy to compute and can be simulated numerically. However, a diagrammatic presentation offers more insight into the nature of the equilibrium and is presented in the following section.

5.2 *The occurrence of currency crises*

In this section we focus on the first two periods of production and lending $t = 1, 2$, so that we can analyze the mechanics of the model using simple graphical representation. In particular, we describe the mechanism leading to multiple expectational equilibria and the subsequent possibility of a currency crisis.

5.2.1 *A graphical representation of the model*

Throughout the remaining part of the chapter, we concentrate on the case where the nominal interest rate in period 2, i_2, is maintained constant by monetary policy in subsequent periods.[20] In other words, we implicitly assume that the government follows an *interest rate targeting* or *inflation rate targeting* (π_3 is fixed) policy.[21] In Aghion *et al.* (2004b), we show that this assumption can be relaxed without significantly altering the results.[22] Taking i_2 as given, the mechanics of the model will now be shown to be fully described by two curves in the (E_1, y_2) space: an IPLM ("Interest-Parity-LM")

---

[20] Jeanne (2000b) presents first- and second generation models using a related two-period approach.

[21] Indeed, as shown above, we have:

$$1 + i_2 = (1 + i^*)(1 + \pi_3).$$

[22] For example, suppose that the government targets the rate of money growth z instead, and for simplicity let us take the inflation rate in period 4, π_4, as given; then using the fact that:

$$1 + \pi_3 = (1 + z_3) \frac{m_2^d(y_2, i_2)}{m_3^d(y_3, i_3)}$$

and:

$$1 + i_3 = (1 + i^*)(1 + \pi_4),$$

we can endogeneize i_2 as a function of y_2 and y_3, increasing in y_2 and decreasing in y_3. In particular, by decreasing y_3, a tight monetary policy, that is, an increase in the nominal interest rate i_1, in period 1, will induce an increase in i_2. This in turn will tend to counteract, but only partly so, the positive effects of such a policy on the demand for the domestic currency and therefore on its value relative to the foreign currency (see Aghion *et al.* 2004b).

curve which describes how future (i.e. period 2) expected output y_2 influences the current (i.e. period 1) exchange rate, E_1, and a W (or "Wealth") curve which describes the period 2 output response of credit-constrained entrepreneurs, y_2, to variations in the (end of) period 1 exchange rate.

The IPLM curve is completely standard: it is simply obtained by combining the IP condition (5.1) with the LM equation (5.2) at $t = 2$ (i.e. LM$_2$) in which the period-2 nominal interest rate i_2 is taken as given. Using the PPP assumption $P_2 = E_2^e = E_2$ (the latter equality follows from the absence of shock in period 2) we get:

$$E_1 = \frac{1 + i^*}{1 + i_1} \cdot \frac{M_2^S}{m^d(y_2, i_2)}, \tag{5.8}$$

which provides a negative relationship between E_1 and y_2. This relationship is shown in Figure 5.3 as the IPLM curve.[23] It is easy to see why the IPLM curve slopes down: an increase in (expected) future output y_2 increases the demand for money (i.e. for domestic currency) in period 2, which in turn will naturally generate a nominal currency appreciation in that period, that is, a

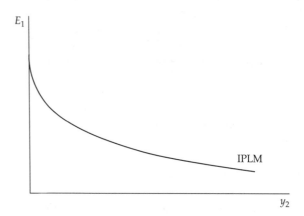

F$_{IG}$. 5.3 IPLM curve.

Source: Aghion *et al.* (2001), figure 2.

[23] Note that our curve differs slightly from the AA curve in Krugman and Obstfeld (2000), which relates E_1 to Y_1 instead of Y_2, and keeps all period 2 variables constant.

reduction in $E_2 = P_2$. The anticipation of a currency appreciation "tomorrow" (i.e. in period 2) increases the attractiveness of holding domestic currency today, and therefore induces a currency appreciation today, that is, a reduction in E_1.

The IPLM curve can be shifted by changes in monetary policy at date $t = 1, 2$. For example, a tight monetary policy which reduces M_1^S or increases i_1 (from 5.4), results in a nominal currency appreciation, that is, a reduction in E_1 for any given y_2. Therefore, a tight monetary policy shifts the IPLM curve downwards. The same occurs with a reduction in M_2^S. These effects are standard: for a given output level, the domestic currency appreciates after a monetary compression in the first period due to a shortage of liquidity and it depreciates after a monetary compression in period 2 due to an expected reduction in inflation. Finally, increases in i_2 also shift the IPLM upward.

The slope of the IPLM curve also depends on how mobile capital is and the extent of substitutability between domestic and foreign currency assets. We have so far assumed perfect mobility and perfect substitutability. Relaxing the first assumption, for example, by introducing the possibility of capital controls, will weaken the relationship between i_1 and E_1. In the extreme case of no capital mobility, the IPLM curve disappears. Relaxing the second assumption introduces a foreign exchange risk premium, a case which is examined at the end of Section 5.2.2. In that case what matters are the factors that determine the premium, such as transaction costs and market thinness.

While the IPLM curve is directly drawn from standard macroeconomic textbooks and holds even when credit markets are perfect, the W curve captures the effect of imperfect credit markets. It is given by equation (5.5):

$$y_2 = f\left(\mu(1-\alpha)\left\{y_1 - (1+r_0)d_1^c - (1+i^*)\frac{E_1}{P_1}(d_1 - d_1^c)\right\}\right). \quad (5.9)$$

At the beginning of period 1, all variables on the right-hand side of (5.9) are fixed except for E_1 (P_1 is given since prices are preset and fixed for the entire period 1).[24] Changes in E_1 (with P_1 fixed) have a negative effect on y_2: an increase in E_1 (a depreciation)

---

[24] The nominal exchange rate E_1, however, has an impact on y_2 when there are deviations from PPP in period 1, that is, if there is an unanticipated shock to

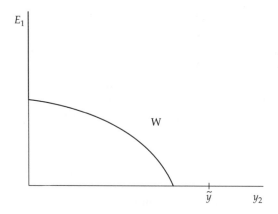

FIG. 5.4 Graphic representation of equation (5.9) yields W curve.
Source: Aghion *et al.* (2001), figure 3.

reduces first period profits Π_1 through an increase in the foreign currency debt burden of domestic entrepreneurs. Representing equation (5.9) (along with the constraint $0 < y_2$) graphically in the (E_1, y_2) space gives us our W curve as depicted in Figure 5.4. The W curve includes an upward segment of the vertical axis when E_1 is such that equation (5.9) yields $y_2 \leq 0$. In the following subsection, we show that under certain conditions the economy summarized by this graphical representation, has two "locally stable"equilibria and argue that the process of switching from the "good"equilibrium to the "bad"equilibrium can be naturally interpreted as a currency crisis.

To conclude this section let us briefly compare our model with a standard open macro model. On the one hand, such a model would include the same kind of IPLM relationship between expected output and the current nominal exchange rate, but on the other hand: (i) our downward-sloping W curve would be replaced by an upward-sloping IS curve (with entrepreneurs' output decisions being constrained by aggregate demand instead of being constrained by current wealth); (ii) our price rigidity assumption would be replaced by some kind of a Phillips curve that would

fundamentals or to expectations such that $E_1 \neq P_1$. The W curve has in common with the Phillips curve that it is vertical in the absence of unanticipated shocks.

determine the rate of price adjustment as a function of the other variables of the model. The fact that the W curve slopes down is of course key to our analysis. Consequences of relaxing this assumption will be discussed later. The value of making specific assumptions about price rigidity rather than adopting an omnibus Phillips curve approach is that it makes clear why different degrees of rigidity can have very different implications for the optimal monetary response to currency crises.

5.2.2 Equilibrium

For a given future path of inflation or nominal interest rates, the equilibrium values of E_1 and y_2, are determined by the two equations, (5.1) at $t = 1$ and (5.5), in which i_2 is taken as given. In other words, the short-run equilibrium of the model is simply defined by the intersection of the IPLM and W curves. As shown in Figure 5.5, there are three possible outcomes. Figure 5.5(a) shows a "good"case with high output and a low exchange rate value as the unique equilibrium. Figure 5.5b shows a "bad"case, where the unexpected currency depreciation is so large that it drives profits and therefore period 2 output to zero.[25] Finally, Figure 5.5c shows an "intermediate"case with multiple equilibria, where only the two extreme equilibria are stable. We will refer to the stable equilibrium with low output and a depreciated domestic currency (i.e. a high E_1 at E^{**}) as the "currency crisis" equilibrium.

The reason for multiple equilibria is simple: if a large currency depreciation is expected, consumers will reduce their money demand because expected output is lower. This in turn leads to a currency depreciation, confirming the consumers' expectations. On the other hand, if no large depreciation is expected, it will not occur in equilibrium because in this case domestic consumers will not reduce their demand for the domestic currency.

Sufficient conditions for having a multiplicity of equilibria require the W curve intersecting the y_2 axis below the IPLM

---

[25] A zero level of output is obviously an extreme simplification. In a more general framework, firms would gain competitiveness through a currency depreciation. Moreover, output would remain positive for firms without foreign currency debt.

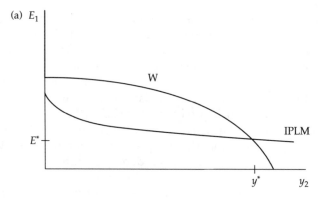

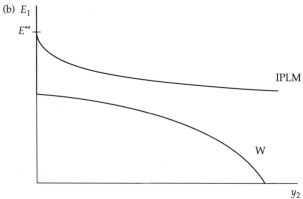

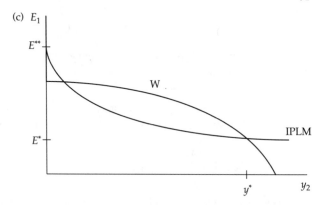

FIG. 5.5 Short-run equilibrium of the model (a) "good" case,
(b) "bad" case, (c) "intermediate" case.

Source: Aghion *et al.* (2001), figure 4.

curve.[26] A currency crisis of this type can be set off by a variety of factors. In the case where there are actually multiple equilibria, the crisis could be brought on by a pure expectational shift. If everyone believes that there will be crisis, then a crisis occurs.[27]

On the other hand, in the case where the initial configuration is as in Figure 5.5(a), only shocks to fundamentals can bring on a crisis. In this case a small fall in productivity (a shift in the $f(\cdot)$ function) or a slight tightening of the credit market (a shift in μ) can shift the W curve down and shift the economy from a configuration of the kind depicted in Figure 5.5(a), to the one depicted figure 5.5(c). This, in turn, can start off a crisis if people expect the "bad" equilibrium. Such a process is illustrated in Figure 5.6. The initial equilibrium is at (y^0, E^0). The negative shock leads to a currency depreciation,

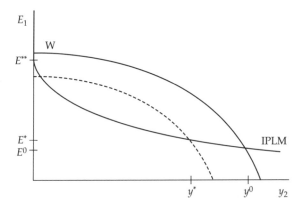

FIG. 5.6 Shock to fundamentals with possible currency crisis.
Source: Aghion *et al.* (2001), figure 5.

[26] A sufficient condition for multiple equilibria including a "currency crisis" equilibrium, is that: $(E_1/P_1)_{y_2=0,W} < (E_1/P_1)_{y_2=0,IPLM}$, or equivalently:

$$\frac{y_1 - (1+r_0)d_1^c}{(1+i^*)(d_1 - d_1^c)} < \frac{1+i^*}{1+i_1}\frac{M_2^s}{P_1}\frac{1}{m^d(0,i_2)}.$$

[27] It is possible to show that these multiple outcomes can also occur when expectational shifts are taken into account when setting prices (formally, in Aghion *et al.* (2004b) we derive sufficient conditions for the existence of nondegenerate sunspots equilibria).

either to (y^*, E^*) or in the worst case to $(0, E^{**})$. The latter case corresponds to a currency crisis situation.

Similarly, suppose that, due to a substantial increase in the perceived exchange rate risk the country now has to pay a risk premium on bonds denominated in its currency. In this case the interest-parity equation (5.1) becomes:

$$1 + i_t = (1 + i^*)\frac{E_2}{E_1} + \eta,$$

where η is the foreign exchange risk premium after the shock.[28]

This increase in risk shifts the IPLM curve upwards, as the new IPLM equation becomes:

$$E_1 = \frac{1 + i^*}{1 + i_1 - \eta}\frac{M_2^s}{m^d(y_2, i_2)}.$$

Starting from a "good case" situation with only one equilibrium with low E_1 and high y_2, this upward shift in IPLM may again lead to a multiple equilibria situation, and therefore to the possibility of a currency crisis. This possibility is actually reinforced by the fact that an increase in the foreign exchange premium raises the interest rate on foreign borrowing which in turn will tend to move the W curve downward.

Similar effects would also follow from an increase in country risk. This leads to an increase in the interest rates faced by domestic entrepreneurs both with regard to domestic and foreign currency debt obligations. An increase in the country risk premium would thus shift the W curve downward without affecting the IPLM curve. In the next section we examine the effects of shocks induced by fiscal and/or monetary policy.

5.3 Policy

It is worth pausing at this point and noting that the mechanism generating a currency crisis in this chapter departs from most existing models of currency crises, as it relies entirely upon private

---

[28] In general, the magnitude of the foreign exchange risk premium η is likely to increase with transaction costs and market thinness.

sector behavior. By contrast, both the "first generation"and the "second generation"models generate currency crises in the case of a fixed exchange rate economy, based upon expectations about the policy regime. Our analysis so far shows that currency crises may also occur in a (credit-constrained) economy with flexible exchange rates and moreover, does not require us to refer to distortions in government policy.

This does not imply that our approach of currency crises cannot be linked to previous theories: as we shall try to argue in this section, it complements previous explanations, for example, by Krugman (1979) or Obstfeld (1994). In Subsection 5.3.1, we analyze an explicitly fixed exchange rate regime, while in Subsection 5.3.2 we briefly consider the government's balance sheet constraint and its interaction with private firms.

5.3.1 Exchange rates regimes

To illustrate the fact that the specific exchange rate regime is not the most crucial element in the analysis, we now consider the case of an economy with an (initially) *fixed* exchange rate system. While such a system can maintain a stable exchange rate when the economy is hit by *small* shocks, the initial exchange rate regime has little influence in preventing a currency crisis following a *large* shock.

In a fixed exchange rate system, the role of the central bank's international reserves, as well as the rule leading to the abandonment of the fixed rate, need to be specified. Fixing the exchange rate in our model implies a given path of money supply in all periods $t > 1$, possibly through the use of international reserves; furthermore, it implies that at date $t = 1$, the central bank can no longer use the interest rate i_1 as a policy instrument, if the interest parity condition is to hold perfectly.[29] More formally, assume that the exchange rate is initially fixed at $E_t = \overline{E}$. Then, the PPP and interest parity conditions imply that the monetary equilibrium

---

[29] With imperfect subtitutability between domestic and foreign assets, the central bank has more flexibility in defending the currency and changing i_1. For large shocks, however, this does not make the analysis significantly different from the full substitutability case.

equation (5.2) in period 2 can be rewritten as:

$$M_2^S = \overline{E} \cdot m^d(y_2, i^*) \tag{5.10}$$

where money supply M_2^S is now endogenous. On the other hand, equilibrium of the central bank's balance sheet imposes the condition :

$$M_2^S = DC_2 + IR_2 \tag{5.11}$$

where DC_2 is domestic credit, typically claims on the government, and IR_2 represents international reserves expressed in domestic currency in period 2.

To understand why a large real shock may force a government to abandon the fixed exchange rate regime and can precipitate the occurrence of a currency crisis, assume that international reserves cannot fall below some floor level $\overline{IR}$, in line with the first generation literature (e.g. Krugman 1979); and that DC_2 is fixed at some level $\overline{DC}$. This situation can be depicted in Figure 5.7.

Suppose that initially, before the shock, the economy is in the good equilibrium described by the intersection between the two curves $IPLM_0$ and W_0 (point A). Then, let $\overline{IPLM}$ denote the lowest IPLM curve consistent with a fixed exchange rate at $E \leq \overline{E}$; this corresponds to a money supply equal to: $M_2^S = \overline{DC} + \overline{IR}$. Finally, let B denote the point on that curve which corresponds exactly to the nominal exchange rate $\overline{E}$. In other words, the parity $E = \overline{E}$ can be maintained only if output y_2 is at least equal to its value at point B.[30]

Now, suppose that a large negative productivity or trade shock shifts the W curve downward (from W_0 to W_1). Clearly, after the shock it becomes impossible to sustain the parity $\overline{E}$ since the W_1 curve intersects the horizontal line $E = \overline{E}$ to the left of B. This implies that the fixed exchange rate $\overline{E}$ has to be abandoned, which in turn may lead the economy to the "bad" equilibrium C defined by the intersection between W_1 and $\overline{IPLM}$ in Figure 5.7.[31]

---

[30] Notice that the analysis can also be conducted in terms of the "shadow" exchange rate as often done in the literature. The intervention of the $\overline{IPLM}$ curve with the W curve gives the shadows exchange rate $\widehat{E}$. As long as $\widehat{E} < \overline{E}$, the fixed exchange rate can be maintained.

[31] Note that once the fixed exchange rate is abandoned, the IPLM curve is likely to be shifted by changes in interest rates. A restrictive monetary policy will increase

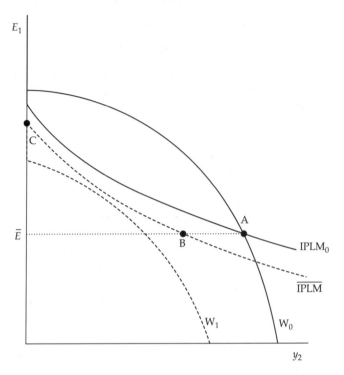

Fig. 5.7 A large real shock may trigger a currency crisis in a fixed exchange rate system.
Source: Aghion *et al.* (2001), figure 6.

It is important to note that the decline in reserves that triggers the currency crisis is caused here by the underlying weakness in the financial health of private firms and not by a fiscal deficit as in the first generation models of currency crises. This does not mean that government behavior and public deficits cannot also have an effect on the occurrence of currency crises, as we will argue in the next subsection. Thus, the potential sources of currency crises highlighted in first generation models, can also be

---

i_1 and shift IPLM down. However, the IPLM may still shift up thereafter due to an increase in i_2, which itself is caused by the expectation of a further depreciation (as in Krugman 1979).

shown to be relevant when analyzed in the context of the "third generation"model in this chapter.

Similarly, we can use our framework to analyze credibility aspects of the kind emphasized by the second generation of currency crises models. For example, instead of assuming a floor level of international reserves, suppose that the government's objective is to minimize a loss function which increases both with the size of output declines and the extent of a currency devaluation. Then, if output depends negatively on the *nominal* interest rate as will be discussed in Section 5.4, we can easily re-obtain the multiple equilibrium result of the second generation models.[32] To see this, note first that an increase in the high interest rate i_0 reduces output y_2 and therefore increases the likelihood of a currency depreciation in period 1. Thus, if at date 0 investors increase their expectation of a currency devaluation in period 1, the interest parity condition in period 0 implies that i_0 must increase, but this in turn will cause an output fall, thereby making the expectation of a currency depreciation self-fulfilling.

Two conclusions can be drawn from these illustrations. First, our model also explains currency crises in economies with an initially fixed exchange rate. Second, first- and second generation features can interact with the balance sheets of private firms and thereby lead to a currency crisis through the same basic mechanism as above.

What does our model tell us about the optimal exchange rate regime? In the case of large shocks, we have just argued that the outcome is likely to be quite similar under a fixed or a floating exchange rate regime. However, this conclusion would change if a government could credibly commit to *never* abandon a given exchange rate parity, for example by instituting a currency board or some kind of dollarization policy. Nevertheless, these strategies are not without risks. One potential drawback of maintaining a fixed exchange rate regime over a long period, for example, through establishing a currency board, is the fact that combined with persistent price rigidity it can lead to currency overvaluation (i.e. to real appreciation, as argued by Calvo and Vegh 1999); this, in turn, may further squeeze firms' profits and thereby add to the

---

[32] Bensaid and Jeanne (1997) present a reduced-form second generation model with an explicit cost of high nominal interest rates leading to multiple equilibria.

difficulty of maintaining a fully credible fixed exchange rate policy. Second, a fixed exchange rate may lead to an increase in the proportion of foreign currency debt and therefore to a more negative slope of the W curve; this, in turn, may add to the difficulty of maintaining a fully credible fixed exchange rate policy.[33] Finally, full dollarization (i.e. giving up the domestic currency and using the foreign currency for all transactions) would obviously avoid a currency crisis. However, the elimination of crises should be weighted against the potential costs of abandoning the domestic currency.[34] A full analysis of the costs and benefits of dollarization is left for future research.

5.3.2 *Public versus private debt in currency crises*

In the first generation of currency crises models, it is the inconsistency between public sector behavior and a fixed exchange rate that is at the source of a crisis. In this subsection, we emphasize the interaction between fiscal variables and the private sector. This interaction can take two forms. First, a fiscal shock such as an increase in government expenditure or a decline in tax revenues, may crowd out the private sector and thereby lead to a currency crisis. Second, a negative shock to fundamentals or to expectations may affect both the private and the public sector in such a way that the deterioration of the private sector's financial health is exacerbated by the deterioration of the public budget.

To organize thoughts it is useful to look at a consolidated government's balance sheet. Assume that government activities are

---

[33] The impact of the exchange rate regime on the currency composition of debt, however, is still not well understood (see Eichengreen and Hausman 1999, for a discussion).

[34] For example, suppose that the domestic country is subject to idiosyncratic shocks, or more generally to shocks that are asymmetrically—or at least imperfectly—correlated with shocks in the foreign currency area, and that domestic prices are sticky (e.g. fixed for two periods or more). Then, not giving up the domestic currency would allow the domestic country to implement countercyclical policies, for example to increase E in a fixed exchange rate regime or to reduce i in a flexible exchange rate regime, in order to reduce the real interest rate and/or to increase the real exchange rate and thereby to prevent a big recession following a large negative shock. This is particularly relevant if competitiveness effects of the kind analyzed above, are significant.

such that in each period t we have:

$$P_t(g_t - t_t) + \left[x^G(1 + i_{t-1}) + (1 - x^G)(1 + i^*)\frac{E_t}{E_{t-1}} \right] P_{t-1} d_t^G$$
$$= P_t d_{t+1}^G + P_t s_t, \tag{5.12}$$

where g_t and t_t denote real expenditure and revenue; d_t^G is the privately held public debt contracted in period $t - 1$ and due to be reimbursed in period t; x^G denotes the fraction of government debt which is in domestic currency; and s_t represents real seigniorage revenue. If the exchange rate were fixed, we would also need to add the change in the central bank's international reserves, but for simplicity we only consider the floating exchange rate case in this subsection. If we divide (5.12) by P_t and assume that PPP holds at $t - 1$, we get the budget constraint in real terms:

$$g_t - t_t + \left[x^G(1 + r_{t-1}) + (1 - x^G)(1 + i^*)\frac{E_t}{P_t} \right] d_t^G = d_{t+1}^G + s_t, \tag{5.13}$$

The first important point that emerges from equation (5.13) is that public sector's debt is affected negatively by unanticipated currency depreciations in exactly the same way as private sector's debt.[35] Thus, it is not difficult to imagine a "second generation" model (e.g. in the line of Obstfeld 1994) where multiple equilibria and the possibility of currency crises, stem from a high proportion of public foreign currency debt. This is in sharp contrast with the existing literature (again, see Obstfeld 1994) where currency crises occur in economies with high proportions of *domestic* currency debt and where having foreign currency debt can help avoid a crisis altogether. Behind this contrast lies the fact that previous models would typically assume *ex post* PPP and no foreign price uncertainty, which implies that foreign currency bonds are a perfect hedge against currency fluctuations. The experience with countries issuing foreign currency

---

[35] Notice that throughout the chapter we consider only short-term (one period) debt. To the extent that the government can have longer maturities than the private sector, it may be less sensitive to exchange rate depreciations.

debt, such as Mexico with its dollar-linked *tesobonos*, tends to support the view that public *foreign* currency debt is not always a stabilizing influence.

Let us now turn to the interaction between the private and the public sector. Consider for example an increase in the primary fiscal deficit at time one, $g_1 - t_1$.[36] The impact on the private sector depends on which other variable adjusts in (5.13). First, assume that an increase in the deficit is financed by an increase in seigniorage s_1. This implies an increase in money growth from period 2 on, which in particular means an increase in M_2^S and in i_2 (due to an increase in π_3). In our graphical analysis, this implies that the IPLM curve will shift upward, which in turn can push the economy from a "good"into a "currency crisis"equilibrium. Interestingly, as in "first generation"models, the proximate cause of the crisis is a budget deficit financed by future inflation. The mechanism behind the crisis, however, is quite different since it is not the currency attack on the fixed exchange rate, but rather the deteriorating financial health of private firms, which causes the crisis.

Now, suppose that the increased budget deficit leads to a reduction in the amount of lending to firms, through a decline in the credit-multiplier μ. This may be due to some standard crowding out between public and private debt; or because a larger deficit would reduce the amount of government funds available to save insolvent or illiquid banks or firms from bankruptcy.[37] This decline in μ will lead to a downward shift of the W curve, which again may result in the possibility of a crisis. Here again, a negative shock on the public sector leads to a crisis through its impact on private firms.

To summarize our discussion in this section, we have argued that although a currency crisis may be directly triggered by a weakening of private sector firms' balance sheets, it can also be provoked by imbalances in the public sector. This may help explain crises episodes like Brazil in the late 1990s, where the corporate and banking sectors suffered from the increasing fiscal imbalances.

---

[36] This increase could be an exogenous change in fiscal policy or an endogenous decline in tax revenue due to some negative shock affecting domestic output.

[37] Aghion *et al.* (2004b) analyze this case, by introducing commercial banks and their reserve and capital requirements explicitly into the framework.

5.3.3 *Monetary policy*

The appropriate monetary policy response to the recent crises has been a hotly debated issue. Our model, being an explicitly monetary model, is well suited as a framework for discussing these issues.[38] Consider the model developed in Sections 5.1 and 5.2. Suppose it is known that the economy has a significant chance of switching to the currency crisis equilibrium, either because of a shift in expectations or because of a real shock. In other words, we are now in a situation such as the one depicted in Figure 5.5(c). Can the monetary authorities do anything that would guarantee that the economy avoids a currency crisis?

Obviously what they need to do is to shift the IPLM curve so that the economy moves to a configuration of the type shown in Figure 5.5(a). Figure 5.8 shows this case. The correct policy response in this case is obviously to increase the interest rate i_1 and/or decrease M_2^S so that the IPLM curve shifts downward.

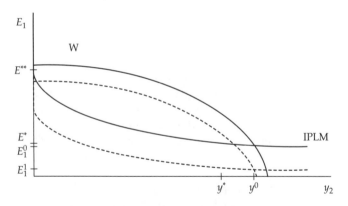

FIG. 5.8 Currency crisis can be avoided by using tight monetary policy.
Source: Aghion *et al.* (2001), figure 7.

---

[38] This section summarizes some of the findings of Aghion *et al.* (2004b). Notice that we do not examine the interaction between monetary policy and the credibility of the authorities (e.g. see Drazen 1999, for such an analysis). See Goldfajn and Baig (1998), Goldfajn and Gupta (1999), and Kray (2000) for empirical analyses of this issue and Lahiri and Vegh (2000) and Flood and Jeanne (2000) for other theoretical analyses.

Figure 5.8 thus shows a situation in which the currency crisis can be avoided and initial output be restored, through appreciating the currency to E_1^1. This can be seen as the standard case for a tight monetary policy during a currency crisis.

The main argument of those defending a lax monetary policy, however, is that interest rate increases negatively affect output. To take this into consideration, we consider a model of the credit market, developed in the Appendix, where credit depends negatively on the real interest rate, that is, $m(r_t)$ with $m' < 0$. To see how this additional effect modifies the W curve we have to take account of the relationship between the real interest rate and the exchange rate. Using the interest parity condition and the definition of the real interest rate, we have: $1 + r_1 = (1 + i^*)P_1/E_1$. This allows us to rewrite the credit multiplier as $m_t = m(E_1/P_1)$, where $m' > 0$.[39] Equation (5.5) then gets re-expressed in the form:

$$y_2 = f\left(\left(1 + m\left(\frac{E_1}{P_1}\right)\right)(1 - \alpha)\left\{y_1 - (1 + r_0)d_1^c\right.\right.$$
$$\left.\left.-(1 + i^*)\frac{E_1}{P_1}(d_1 - d_1^c)\right\}\right). \tag{5.14}$$

Changes in E_1 (with P_1 fixed) have now two effects on y_2. In addition to an increase in the foreign currency debt burden of domestic entrepreneurs, an increase in E_1 reduces the real interest rate r_1, which in turn relaxes the credit constraint and therefore increases the availability of funds d_2 at the beginning of period 2. The slope of the W curve depends on the relative importance of the two effects. Figure 5.4, with μ constant, represents the case where the foreign currency debt effect dominates. In Figure 5.9 the relationship between y_2 and E_1 is positive. It becomes a vertical line at $\tilde{y}$ when μ is so large (r_1 so small) that the credit constraint is no longer binding. Note that other shapes of the W curve are possible. In particular, it might be positively sloped for low values of E_1 and negatively sloped for high values of E_1.

---

[39] The m function is increasing in E_1/P_1, since a high value of E_1/P_1 predicts that future inflation will be high relative to future depreciation, and therefore depresses the real interest rate.

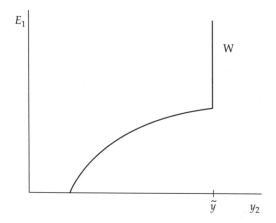

FIG. 5.9 The slope of the W curve if credit constraint effect dominates.
Source: Aghion *et al*. (2001), figure 8.

The exact expression for the slope of the W curve (from equation (5.14) is:

$$\frac{d(E_1/P_1)}{dy_2} = 1/f'\left(s\frac{\Pi_1}{P_1}\right)s\left[\frac{m'}{1+m}\frac{\Pi_1}{P_1} - (1+i^*)\left(d_1 - d_1^c\right)\right]$$

where $s = (1 - \alpha)(1 + m)$. It is clear from this expression that when there is no foreign currency debt, that is, when $d_1^c = d_1$, the W curve is always upward-sloping. As the proportion of foreign currency debt increases, the slope of the W curve increases, turning negative; the limit is achieved at $d_1^c = 0$. When credit markets are completely absent, that is, when $m = 0$, we must have $d_1^c = d_1 = 0$ and therefore the W curve would always be vertical. This is as it should be: when there is no credit, exchange rate variations should not affect investment capacity. The W curve is also vertical when m is very large and therefore the credit constraint is not binding: in this case output should not be affected by the profitability of the firm sector. In the intermediate case where there is a substantial amount of borrowing but the credit constraint still binds, the W curve can be downward-sloping and relatively flat.[40] This turns out to be the case where we can have currency crises. In that sense currency crises will be associated with countries that are at an intermediate level of financial development.

Let us now examine monetary policy where the W curve slopes up as in Figure 5.10(a). In this case, consider a negative shock that

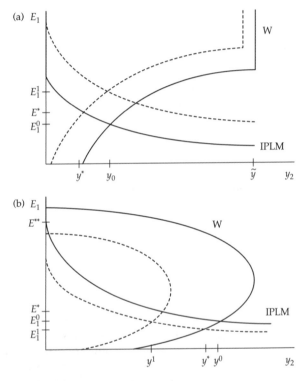

FIG. 5.10 Monetary policy where the W curve (a) slopes up, (b) has both a positive and a negative slope.

Source: Aghion *et al.* (2001), figure 9.

[40] What happens between $m = 0$ and the nonbinding credit constraint is rather complex since each of the terms $f'(\cdot), m'/(1 + m)$, and $d_1 - d^c$ depend on the m function. In particular, the specific way in which we have modeled the credit market and the decision to borrow in foreign currency plays an important role and for this reason we have chosen not to discuss these aspects in detail.

has reduced output from y^0 to y^* and caused a currency depreciation from E_1^0 to E^*. Then, an expansionary monetary policy, that is, a decrease in i_1 or an increase in M_2^S, can help us maintain the initial level of output, y^0, though such policy will shift the IPLM curve upward and therefore induce a further currency depreciation to E_1^1. Notice, however, that there is no crisis, either potential or actual, in this case. The case where the W curve slopes down is the same as the one analyzed in Figure 5.8, so that an interest rate increase can avoid a currency crisis. Finally, there may still be more complex situations where the W curve has both a positive and a negative slope, as in Figure 5.10(b). In that case a leftward shift in the W curve following a negative shock may again lead to multiple equilibria and a potential crisis. While the optimal monetary policy is now restrictive it can only eliminate the risk of a currency crisis at the cost of reducing aggregate output down to y_1^1.

To summarize, as in the extended model with competitiveness effects, an expansionary policy can be justified *only in situations where the W curve is upward-sloping, that is, only if currency crises are impossible*. The intuition behind this claim is as follows: the effect of lowering nominal interest rates can be beneficial in this model only if lowering nominal interest rates also lowers real interest rates, which in turn raises μ and has an expansionary effect on output.[41] Now, the only way to lower real interest rates in our model, is to allow the currency to slide down so that the expected future appreciation of the domestic currency can compensate bond holders for the lower interest rate. But allowing the currency to slide in a crisis-prone economy will cause output to contract (this is precisely what makes the economy crisis prone) and this output contraction in turn will lead to further depreciation of the local currency and push the economy closer to a crisis. Therefore a currency crisis in our model demands a tight monetary policy.[42]

---

[41] However, in Aghion *et al.* (2004b) we argue that it can be counterproductive for the central bank to be tough both, on money supply and on the rate it charges at the discount window for banks that need immediate cash.

[42] Aghion *et al.* (2004b) analyze the output impact of tight monetary policy in the medium term, that is, in period 3.

5.4 Conclusion

In this chapter we have developed a simple framework to study currency crises and assess the effects of monetary policy. This "third generation"model is particularly well-suited to analyze the case of economies such as those in Asia, where the source of currency crises lay primarily in the deteriorating balance sheets of private domestic firms and commercial banks rather than in uncontrolled budget deficit policies by local governments (e.g., see Mishkin 1999).

Three main conclusions emerged from our analysis. First, an economy with a large proportion of foreign currency debt is more likely to face currency crises associated with large recessions and currency devaluations; but the presence of large competitiveness effects will instead decrease the likelihood of a crisis. Second, a currency crisis may occur both under a fixed or a flexible exchange rate regime as the primary source of such a crisis is the deteriorating balance sheet of private firms. Third, public sector imbalances can have destabilizing effects on the domestic currency through the crowding out effects of public debt (especially public foreign currency debt) on the balance sheet and credit access of private firms.

A natural next step if this framework is to be used for policy purposes, is to empirically assess the relative importance of the various effects pointed out in the chapter. In particular, we need to learn more on the determination of *actual foreign currency debt ratios*, and also on the relative speeds of price versus interest rate adjustments as our analysis suggests that the optimal design of monetary policy, is potentially sensitive to the degree of price stickiness, or more precisely to the duration of the deviation from PPP following the initial shock.

Appendix: The Credit Multiplier

The credit multiplier m_t is derived, as in Aghion *et al.* (1999b), from *ex post* moral hazard considerations. Namely, suppose that domestic entrepreneurs can either produce transparently and fully repay their loan or instead can hide their production in order to default on their debt repayment obligations. There is a nominal cost to hiding, which is proportional to the amount of funds invested: cP_tk_t. Yet, whenever the entrepreneur chooses to default, the lender can still collect his due repayment with probability p. Thus, the borrower will decide not to default if and only if:

$$P_ty_t - (1 + i_{t-1})P_{t-1}d_t \geq P_ty_t - cP_tk_t - p(1 + i_{t-1})P_{t-1}d_t,$$

where the left-hand side (resp. right-hand side) is the borrower's net expected revenue if she repays (resp. if she defaults on) her debt. Then, the above incentive constraint can be rewritten as: $d_t \leq m_tw_t$, where:

$$m_t = m(r_{t-1}) = \frac{c}{[(1-p)(1+r_{t-1}) - c]}.$$

The multiplier m_t is increasing in the monitoring probability p (which in turn reflects the level of financial development of the economy) and it is decreasing in the real interest rate r_{t-1}. The currency composition of debt does not affect m_t since lending is determined before any shock occurs, that is at a time where both the PPP and the interest parity conditions hold.

Conclusion

Some basic themes

A common theme throughout these lectures is that, by looking at the economy through the lens of private entrepreneurs who invest under credit constraints, one can go a long way toward explaining persistent macroeconomic volatility and the effects of volatility on growth. In particular, in Chapter 2 we argued that volatility becomes detrimental to growth when it forces credit-constrained entrepreneurs to sacrifice long-term productivity-enhancing investments during slumps, and that the lower the degree of financial development of an economy, the more negative the effect of aggregate volatility on long-run growth. In Chapters 3 and 4 we turned our attention to the reverse causal channel: from growth to volatility. There, we analyzed how growing economies with credit-constrained entrepreneurs could experience persistent volatility or amplified shocks due to the interplay between credit constraints and the rise in interest rates or real exchange rates occurring during a boom. We also argued that this "credit channel" approach is strongly supported by recent empirical studies on lending booms and crises in emerging market economies and also by recent US volatility history, at least between the Second World War and the early 1990s.

However, our purpose was not only to better explain macro-economic volatility and its impact on growth, but also to recruit our readers to a new, wide open research program on the macropolicy of growth. Taking stock of the limitations of previous attempts based on the AK model, we argued that a more Schumpeterian approach that would take entrepreneurs as the unit of analysis had the potential to deliver new interesting insights on the effects of various budgetary or monetary policies on aggregate output and growth. For example, our analysis in Chapters 2 and 3 suggested that less financially developed economies should benefit more from countercyclical budgetary policies. Interestingly, EU countries that are less financially developed than the United States, partly as a consequence of the Maastricht Treaty and its Stability and Growth Pact, follow far less countercyclical budgetary policies than the United States. Our analysis in Chapter 4 pointed to a stabilizing role of FDI and a potentially destabilizing effect of financial liberalization primarily focused on opening lending markets before improving credit monitoring or encouraging FDI. And our analysis in Chapter 5 pointed to the complex effects of increasing interest rates in response to a currency crisis, again suggesting that policy recommendations should be based on (third generation) macromodels that fully explore and integrate the microeconomic characteristics of private sector firms.[1] Thus, far from closing a domain, this book is just the first step of what we hope will develop into a whole research project on macroeconomic policy and growth in economies subject to aggregate volatility.

Looking forward: from credit markets to stock markets

One final remark to conclude. We argued above that the analysis in Chapters 3 and 4 fits the US case relatively well up until the 1990s: in particular, toward the end of a boom, US firms would always experience sharp increases in their leverage ratios, in the interest rates spreads between short- and long-term bonds or between bonds and (short-term) commercial paper, in default rates and in the real exchange rate, after which the economy would enter a slump. However, in the recession of the late 1990s–early 2000s, there was no such tightening of credit markets. In fact when we gave these lectures in early 2000, the lack of a sharp increase in leverage ratios and in the interest rate spread during the late 1990s had led us to venture the prediction that no true recession should occur during the following two or three years: The point was that none of the credit indicators mentioned in Chapter 3 or 4 had turned red. In retrospect it is clear where we went wrong: the

---

[1] See Aghion *et al.* (2004b) for a policy analysis based on a fully microfounded model of the monetary sector, where the government or central bank can decide upon both, the nominal interest rate and "discount window" policies to refinance commercial banks.

problems came not from firms' debt build up, but from the stock market. Thus, in order to explain the recent boom and bust episode in the United States, one should turn attention to models of the stock market.

There is a whole literature on stock market-driven volatility. First, there are a number of seminal papers on the macroeconomic consequences of irrational speculation, for example by Malkiel (1985) and Kindleberger (1978). More recently, Blanchard (1979) and others have reinterpreted speculative bubbles and their outburst as rational phenomena associated with multiple expectational equilibria and the existence of sunspots. None of these explanations, however, directly help us in understanding why there was a crisis in an economy like the United States which was not only growing fast, but also had exceptionally high productivity growth.

Therefore, let us sketch an approach to booms and crashes that gives a central role to technical progress and the expansion of new markets. In an interesting recent paper, Zeira (1999), makes the following simple point: In a world where things are growing and no one knows exactly how big the market is, the natural tendency for investors is to keep going till the limit is hit. A crash is therefore the natural concomittant of the growth of new markets.

Zeira's model is attractively simple and it also sounds right, especially in its linking of stock market booms and crashes to the opening and expansion of new markets. Yet, a few questions remain unanswered. In particular, the capacity threshold X and the corresponding saturation time T are assumed to be deterministic. Would the crash still obtain if these were random instead? Also, a stock market crash in this model does not translate into an output slump: all that happens in this model, is that output stops growing when the capacity limit X is reached. Finally, the model explains overshooting, not undershooting. But in order to generate permanent fluctuations in aggregate output, one may need both.

A second explanation, which is based upon recent work by Aghion and Stein (2004), emphasizes coordination problems between firms and the stock market. In particular, firms' desire to "please the market" and to allocate effort to match what they believe to be market's expectations leads firms to delay the necessary shift from a growth strategy (whereby sales maximization should be the paramount objective) to a margin strategy (whereby cost minimization should become the dominant criterion for good management) as the market demand for their product gets saturated. In contrast to our discussion in Chapter 4 on the stabilizing effect of equity investment, in Aghion and Stein (2004) it is the very existence of a stock market and managers' responsiveness to stock market incentives, which drives volatility and the occurrence of booms and busts.

The basic idea of Aghion and Stein (2004) can be summarized as follows. Consider firms in a new expanding sector. Firm managers are assumed to face a multitask effort allocation problem at any period in time. More specifically, managers have limited attention which they must allocate between two competing tasks, each of which contributes to profit maximization. A first task is to maximize sales (or sales growth), and we use the expressions "sales strategy" or "growth strategy" to refer to managers that invest all their effort in maximizing sales. A second task is to minimize costs, and we use the expression "margin strategy" to refer to managers that put all their emphasis on minimizing production costs and thereby maximizing profit margins for given output volume.

Next, let us assume that performance at either of these two tasks depends in a multiplicative way upon managerial effort at this task and upon an ability parameter which is unknown to all agents as in Holmstrom's (1999) model of managerial incentives. Then, as a new market opens up and starts expanding, firms' managers in that sector will first choose to emphasize sales and growth in order to take advantage of the unfilled demand for the new product. The stock market will correctly anticipate such an allocation of effort by managers, and consequently its investors will use their observation of sales performance to update their beliefs on managerial ability. However, at some point, when demand for the new product is almost saturated, it becomes efficient for managers to reallocate their effort from sales maximization to cost minimization.

If managers do not respond to stock market incentives and consequently do not care about investors' assessment of their ability, they will shift from a growth to a margin strategy when it is efficient to do so. However, if they care about the stock market and its assessment of managerial talent (e.g. for career concern reasons or simply because they hold stock options whose valuation by the market depends upon investors' information about managerial ability), managers may decide to stick to the growth strategy in order to "please the market," in other words, to give the market what they think it wants from them.

An attentive reader will object that there exists an equilibrium in which the market anticipates a shift from growth to margin, and the managers shift when it becomes efficient to do so. However, what Aghion and Stein show is that before market demand fully saturates, it goes through a region of multiple equilibria in which the above equilibrium coexists with another equilibrium in which the market does not change its expectations about managerial allocation of effort and consequently managers also stick to the growth strategy. Moreover, this latter equilibrium may become unique once we depart from common knowledge, for example, by assuming that the market believes that managers believe that the market is inertial in its conjectures in the sense that it always maintains the same conjecture about managers' strategies as in the previous period if maintaining the same strategy is still an equilibrium of the static game this period. Consequently, although it would have been efficient for firm managers to switch to a margin strategy, they choose to "please the market" by sticking for several more periods to the growth strategy.

Eventually, the market will become so saturated, and the growth strategy so inefficient, that the firm will have no choice but to switch to a margins strategy. But compared to the first-best, the change will come too late, and in an abrupt fashion: namely, firms will go to the other extreme of focusing exclusively on cost-cutting, as opposed to taking a balanced approach of devoting some resources to each of the two strategies. This lack of balance in turn induces another round of fluctuations. Once entrenched in the margins equilibrium, with the market now expecting emphasis on the margins dimension, the firm will neglect growth opportunities for too long, until it gets to a point where it is forced to go back to the growth strategy, at which point the whole process begins again.

We believe that this story captures important aspects of what happened during the recent period in the high-tech sector(s) in the United States. First, there is ample anecdotal evidence pointing at the fact that, during the late 1990s, venture capitalists provided extensive funding to new high-tech startups without barely screening their projects, thereby encouraging those firms to pursue a growth strategy. In the specific case of Amazon.com, Hong and

Stein (2004) document that "through the end of 1999, analysts were almost uniformly focused on growth-related indicators when valuing Amazon stock, at the expense of more profitability or cost-related indicators. Conversely, during the cost-cutting phase that followed, analysts began to focus more on costs measures."

We have just described two attempts at explaining volatility in growing economies where firms are being financed through the stock market. The first story, by Zeira (1999), emphasizes informational overshooting by speculators who ignore the extent of total demand capacity and keep revising their market expectations upwards as long as they have not hit this capacity. The second story, by Aghion and Stein (2004), emphasizes the limited attention of managers (when investing effort in growth- versus margins-enhancing activities), together with their desire to please the stock market and to adapt their effort allocation to what they believe market expectations to be. While the former story may account for stock market fluctuations, the latter story can explain output fluctuations resulting from the interaction between firms and the stock market in newly emerging sectors.

The research agenda remains wide open, but one particular extension that might be worth pursuing in light of this and the previous chapters, is to reintroduce credit market imperfections, and ask to what extent the credit-based mechanisms analyzed in the previous chapter and the stock market mechanism sketched in this chapter, can be mutually reinforcing. This and many other questions we raised throughout these chapters, are left to future research.

References

Aghion, Ph. and P. Howitt (1992), "A model of Growth through Creative Destruction," *Econometrica* 60, 323–351.

Aghion, Ph. and P. Howitt (1998), *Endogenous Growth Theory*, Cambridge, MA: MIT Press.

Aghion Ph. and J. Stein (2004), "Growth vs. Margins: Business-Cycle Implications of Giving the Stock Market What It Wants," mimeo, Harvard University.

Aghion, Ph., A. Banerjee, and T. Piketty (1999a), "Dualism and Macroeconomic Volatility," *Quarterly Journal of Economics* 114, 1321–1358.

Aghion, Ph., Ph. Bacchetta, and A. Banerjee (1999b), "Capital Markets and the Instability of Open Economies," CEPR Discussion Paper No. 2083.

Aghion, Ph., Ph. Bacchetta, and A. Banerjee (2000), "A Simple Model of Monetary Policy and Currency Crises," *European Economic Review* 44, 728–738.

Aghion, Ph., Ph. Bacchetta, and A. Banerjee (2001), "Currency Crises and Monetary Policy in an Economy with Credit Constraints," *European Economic Review* 45, 1121–1150.

Aghion, Ph., Angeletos, G.-M., A. Banerjee, and K. Manova [AABM] (2004), "Volatility and Growth: Financial Development and the Cyclical Composition of Investment," mimeo, Harvard University and MIT.

Aghion, Ph., Ph. Bacchetta, and A. Banerjee (2004a), "Financial Development and the Instability of Open Economies," *Journal of Monetary Economics* 51, 1077–1106.

Aghion, Ph., Ph. Bacchetta, and A. Banerjee (2004b), "A Corporate Balance-Sheet Approach to Currency Crises," *Journal of Economic Theory* 119, 6–30.

Aghion, Ph., Ph. Bacchetta, R. Ranciere, and K.S. Rogoff [ABRR] (2004), "Productivity Growth and Appropriate Exchange Rate Regimes," mimeo, Harvard University.

Aghion, Ph., R.J. Barro, and I. Marinescu (2004), work in progress on "Countercyclical Budgetary Policy and Growth," Harvard University.

Banerjee, A. and E. Duflo (2004), "Do Firms Want to Borrow More? Testing Credit Constraints Using a Directed Lending Program," BREAD Working Paper No. 005.

Barro, R.J. (1986), "The Behavior of U.S. Deficits," in R.J. Gordon (ed.), *The American Business Cycle: Continuity and Change*, Chicago, IL: University of Chicago Press.

Barro, R.J. and J.W. Lee (1996), "International Measures of Schooling Years and Schooling Quality," *American Economic Review* 86, 218–223.

Bean, C.R. (1990), "Endogenous Growth and the Procyclical Behaviour of Productivity," *European Economic Review* 34, 355–363.

Beaudry, P. (1996), "The Intertemporal Elasticity of Substitution: An Exploration Using a US Panel of State Data," *Economica* 63, 495–512.

Bensaid, B. and O. Jeanne (1997), "The Instability of Fixed Exchange Rate Systems When Raising the Interest Rate is Costly," *European Economic Review* 41, 1461–1478.

Bernanke, B. and M. Gertler (1989), "Agency Costs, Net Worth, and Business Fluctuations," *American Economic Review* 79, 14–31.

Bernanke, B., M. Gertler, and S. Gilchrist (1998), "The Financial Accelerator in a Quantitative Business Cycle Framework," in J. Taylor and M. Woodford (eds), *Handbook of Macroeconomics*, vol. 1C, 1341–1393.

Blanchard, O.J. (1979), "Speculative Bubbles, Crashes and Rational Expectations," *Economics Letters* 3, 387–389.

Blanchard, O.J. (1996), *Macroeconomics*, New Jersey: Prentice Hall.

Bohn, H. (1990), "A Positive Theory of Foreign Currency Debt," *Journal of International Ecomomics* 29, 273–292.

Bruchez, P.-A. (2001), "Discrete and Continuous Time in Financial Accelerator Models," in progress, Study Center Gerzensee.

Bruno, M. (1993), *Crisis, Stabilization and Economic Reform: Therapy by Consensus*, Oxford: Clarendon Press.

Burstein, A., M. Eichenbaum, and S. Rebelo (2004), "Large Devaluations and the Real Exchange Rate," University of California Los Angeles Economics Online Papers 267.

Calvo, G.A. (1998), "Balance of Payments Crises in Emerging Markets: Large Capital Inflows and Sovereign Governments," Paper presented at the NBER Conference on Currency Crises, Cambridge, MA, February.

Calvo, G. and C. Vegh (1999), "Inflation Stabilization and BOP Crises in Developing Countries," in J. Taylor and M. Woodford (eds), *Handbook of Macroeconomics*, vol. 1C, 1531–1614, Amsterdam: North-Holland.

Chamon, M. and R. Hausmann (2002), "Why Do Countries Borrow the Way They Borrow?," Paper presented at conference, Currency and Maturity Matchmaking: Redeeming Debt from Original Sin, 21–22 November, Washington, DC.

Chang, R. and A. Velasco (1999), "Liquidity Crises in Emerging Markets: Theory and Policy," Working Paper 99-15, Federal Reserve Bank of Atlanta.

Cooper, R. (1971), "Currency Devaluation in Developing Countries," Princeton's Essays in International Finance, reproduced in P.B. Kenen (ed.), *The International Monetary System: Highlights from Fifty Years of Princeton's Essays in International Finance*, Boulder, CO and Oxford: Westview Press.

Diamond, D. (1984), "Financial Intermediation and Delegated Monitoring,"*Review of Economic Studies* 62, 393–414.

Drazen, A. (1999), "Interest Rate Defense Against Speculative Attacks Under Asymmetric Information," mimeo, University of Maryland.

Eichengreen, B. (2004), "Financial Instability," in: B. Lomborg (ed), "Global Crises, Global Solutions," Cambridge: Cambridge University Press.

Eichengreen, B. and R. Hausmann (1999), "Exchange Rate and Financial Fragility," paper presented at the Federal Reserve Bank of Kansas City's Conference on Issues in Monetary Policy, August.

Engel, C. (1993), "Real Exchange Rates and Relative Prices: An Empirical Investigation," *Journal of Monetary Economics* 32, 35–50.

Engel, C. (1999), "Accounting for U.S. Real Exchange Rate Changes," *Journal of Political Economy* 107, 507–538.

Falcetti, E. and A. Missale (1999), "The Currency Denomination of Public Debt and the Choice of the Monetary Regime," CEP Discussion Papers 0427, London School of Economics.

Fazzari, S.M., R.G. Hubbard, and B.C. Petersen (1988), "Financing Constraints and Corporate Investment," *Brookings Papers on Economic Activity* 1, 141–195.

Flood, R.P. and O. Jeanne (2000), "An Interest Rate Defense of a Fixed Exchange Rate?," IMF Working Paper 00/159, International Monetary Fund, Washington, DC.

Flood, R.P. and N. Marion (1998), "Perspectives on the Recent Currency Crises Literature," *International Journal of Finance and Economics* 4, 1–26.

Frankel, M. (1962), "The Production Function in Allocation and Growth: A Synthesis," *American Economic Review* 52, 995–1022.

Friedman, B. and K. Kuttner (1993), "Why Does the Paper–Bill Spread Predict Real Economic Activity?," *Business Cycle Indicators and Forecasting*, J. Stock and M. Watson (eds), Chicago, IL: University of Chicago Press, 213–249.

Furman, J. and J.E. Stiglitz (1998), "Economic Crises: Evidence and Insights from East Asia," *Brooking Papers on Economic Activity* 2, 1–135.

Gali, J. and M. Hammour (1991), "Long-run Effects of Business Cycles," Papers 540, Columbia University.

Garber, P. and Svensson L.E. (1995), "The Operation and Collapse of Fixed Exchange Rate Regimes," in G.M. Grossman and K.S. Rogoff (eds), *Handbook of International Economics*, vol. 3, Amsterdam: North-Holland.

Gavin M. and R. Hausmann (1996), "Securing Stability and Growth in a Shock Prone Region: The Policy Challenge for Latin America," InterAmerican Development Bank Working Paper 315.

Ghosh, A., A.-M. Gulde, and H. Wolf (2003), *Exchange Rate Regimes: Choices and Consequences*, Cambridge, MA: MIT Press.

Goldfajn, I. and T. Baig (1998), "Monetary Policy in the Aftermath of Currency Crises: The case of Asia," IMF Working Paper, WP/98/170, December.

Goldfajn, I. and P. Gupta (1999), "Does Monetary Policy Stabilize the Exchange Rate Following a Currency Crisis?," IMF Working Paper, WP/99/42, March.

Goldstein, M. and C. Udry (1999), "Agricultural Innovation and Resource Management in Ghana," mimeo, Yale University.

Gourinchas, P.-O., R. Valdés, and O. Landerretche [GVL] (2001), "Lending Booms: Latin America and the World," *Economia* 1, 47–99.

Griffith-Jones, S. and R. Gottschalk (2004), "Costs of Currency Crises and Benefits of International Financial Reform," mimeo, Institute of Development Studies, Sussex.

Hall, R.E. (1988), "Intertemporal Substitution in Consumption," *Journal of Political Economy* 96, 339–357.

Hall, R.E. (1991). "Recessions as Reorganizations," *NBER Macroeconomics Annual*.

Holmstrom, B.R. (1999), "Managerial Incentive Problems—A Dynamic Perspective," *Review of Economic Studies* 66, 162–182.

Hong, H. and J. Stein (2004), "Simple Forecasts and Paradigm Shifts," mimeo, Harvard University.

Invernizzi, S. and A. Medio (1991), "On Lags and Chaos in Economic Dynamic Models," *Journal of Mathematical Economics* 20, 521–550.

Jeanne, O. (2000a), "Foreign Currency Debt and the Global Financial Architecture," *European Economic Review* 44, 719–727.

Jeanne, O. (2000b), *Currency Crises: A Perspective on Recent Theoretical Developments*, Special Papers in International Economics No. 20, International Finance Section, Princeton University.

Jones, L., R. Manuelli, and E. Stacchetti (2000), "Technology and Policy Shocks in Models of Endogenous Growth," Federal Reserve Bank of Minneapolis Working Paper 281.

Kindleberger, C. (1978), *Manias, Panics and Crashes: A History of Financial Crises*, New York: Basic Books.

King, R.G., C.I. Plosser, and S. Rebelo (1988), "Production, Growth and Business Cycles II: New Directions," *Journal of Monetary Economics* 21, 309–341.

Kray, A. (2000), "Do High Interest Rates Defend Currencies during Speculative Attacks?" mimeo, World Bank.

Krugman, P.R. (1979), "A Model of Balance of Payments Crises," *Journal of Money, Credit and Banking* 11, 311–325.

Krugman, P.R. (1999), "Balance Sheets, The Transfer Problem, and Financial Crises," in P. Isard, A. Razin, and A. Rose (eds), *International Finance and Financial Crises*, Essays in Honor of Robert P. Flood, Kluwer, Dordrecht.

Krugman, P.R. and M. Obstfeld (2000), *International Economics—Theory and Policy*, Addison-Wesley.

Kydland, F. and E. Prescott (1982), "Time to Build and Aggregate Fluctuations," *Econometrica* 50, 1345–1370.

Kyotaki, N. and J. Moore (1997), "Credit Cycles," *Journal of Political Economy* 105, 211–248.

Lahiri, A. and C.A. Végh (2000), "Output Costs, BOP Crises, and Optimal Interest Rate Policy," mimeo, University of California Los Angeles.

Lamont, O. (1997), "Cash Flow and Investment: Evidence from Internal Capital Markets," *Journal of Finance* 52, 83–109.

Levine, R., N. Loyaza, and T. Beck (2000), "Financial Intermediation and Growth: Causality and Causes," *Journal of Monetary Economics* 46, 31–77.

Long, G.B. and C.I. Plosser (1987), "Sectoral vs. Aggregate Shocks in the Business Cycles," *American Economic Review* 77, 333–336.

Malkiel, B.G. (1985), *A Random Walk Down Wall Street*, Cambridge, MA: MIT Press.

McKenzie, D. and C. Woodruff (2003), "Do Entry Costs Provide an Empirical Basis for Poverty Traps? Evidence from Mexican Microenterprises," BREAD Working Paper No. 020.

Mishkin, F.S. (1996), "Understanding Financial Crises: A Developing Country Perspective," *Annual World Bank Conference on Development Economics*, 29–62.

Mishkin, F.S. (1999), "Global Financial Instability: Framework, Events, Issues," *Journal of Economic Perspectives* 13, 3–20.

Obstfeld, M. (1994), "The Logic of Currency Crises," *Cahiers Economiques et Monétaires*, Banque de France 43, 189–213.

Obstfeld, M. and K.S. Rogoff (1995), "Exchange Rate Dynamics Redux," *Journal of Political Economy* 103, 624–660.

Obstfeld, M. and K.S. Rogoff (1996), *Foundations of International Macroeconomics*, Cambridge, MA: MIT Press.

Olley, G.S. and A. Pakes (1996), "The Dynamics of Productivity in the Telecommunications Equipment Industry," *Econometrica* 64, 1263–1297.

Radelet, S. and J. Sachs (1998), "The Onset of the East Asian Financial Crisis," NBER Working Paper No. 6680.

Ramey, G. and V. Ramey (1995), "Cross-Country Evidence on the Link Between Volatility and Growth," *American Economic Review* 85, 1138–1151.

Razin, A., E. Sadka, and C.-W. Yuen (1998), "A Pecking Order of Capital Inflows and International Tax Principles," *Journal of International Economics* 44, 45–68.

Rogoff, K.S., A.M. Husain, A. Mody, R. Brooks, and N. Oomes (2003), "Evolution and Performance of Exchange Rate Regimes," IMF Working Paper 03/243.

Romer, P.M. (1986), "Increasing Returns and Long-Run Growth," *Journal of Political Economy* 94, S1002–S1037.

Romer, P.M. (1990), "Endogenous Technological Change," *Journal of Political Economy* 98, 71–102.

Saint-Paul, G. (1993), "Productivity Growth and the Structure of the Business Cycle," *European Economic Review* 37, 861–883.

Schneider, M. and A. Tornell (2000), "Balance Sheet Effects, Bailout Guarantees and Financial Crises," NBER Working Papers 8060.

Solow, R. (1956), "A Contribution to the Theory of Economic Growth," *Quarterly Journal of Economics* 70, 65–94.

Stock, J. and M. Watson (1997), "Business Cycle Fluctuations in U.S. Macroeconomic Time Series," mimeo, Harvard and Princeton Universities.

Tirole, J. (2002), *Financial Crisis, Liquidity and the International Monetary System*, Princeton: Princeton University Press.

Zeira, J. (1999), "Informational Overshooting, Booms and Crashes," CEPR Discussion Papers 823.

Index